BOOM TOWN BOY

Jack de Yonge

TEMPERATURE
BANK
MODEL

BOOM TOWN BOY

Coming of Age on Alaska's Lost Frontier

Jack de Yonge

EPICENTER PRESS
Alaska Book Adventures™
www.EpicenterPress.com

Epicenter Press is a regional press publishing nonfiction books about the arts, history, environment, and diverse cultures and lifestyles of Alaska and the Pacific Northwest.

Publisher: Kent Sturgis
Acquisitions Editor: Lael Morgan
Editor: Kent Sturgis
Photo research: Rosalie L'Ecuyer
Proofreader: Patricia Sturgis, Melanie Wells
Cover & text design: Victoria Michael
Printer: Thomson-Shore, Inc.

Photos: front cover—author Jack de Yonge, left, as a young boy; Jack's family (from left, his Dad, Jack, his brother, and his mother) sitting on the running board of the family car; back cover—author and canine friend, photo courtesy of Sonjia de Yonge; pages 1-2, Second Avenue, Fairbanks, circa 1945. Credits: unless otherwise credited, photos appearing in *Boom Town Boy* are from the de Yonge family collection, courtesy of the author; page 19 (top), Alaska Steamship Company, UAF Alaska & Polar Regions Collections, ASL-P44-09-035; (bottom), Alaska Steamship Company, Alaska State Library-Historical Collections, ASL-P44-09-035; page 126, Harry T. Becker photographs, Alaska State Library, ASL-P67-135; page 134, (bottom) Anthony J. Dimond Papers, UAF Alaska & Polar Regions Collections, UAF-1992-90-10; page 135, Iches Collection, Alaska Museum of History and Art; page 138, both photos from Kay Kennedy Aviation Photograph Collection, UAF Alaska & Polar Regions Collections, UAF-1991-98-842 (top), UAF-1991-98-868 (bottom).

Library of Congress Control Number: 2010927002
ISBN 978-1-935347-06-4

10 9 8 7 6 5 4 3 2 1
Printed in the United States of America

To order single copies of this title, mail $14.95 plus $6.00 for shipping (WA residents add $1.90 state sales tax) to Epicenter Press, PO Box 82368, Kenmore, WA 98028; call us at 800-950-6663, or visit www.EpicenterPress.com.

To my beloved Sonjia, who for a half-century
has labored to civilize a Fairbanks boy, with fair success,
even if the job isn't done yet.

I would like to thank Kent Sturgis and Lael Morgan of Epicenter Press for fluming out of this book the overburden weighing down my first draft. Washing away the dross is what good editors do. What errors there may be in *Boom Town Boy* I claim as my own and no one else's.

CONTENTS

INTRODUCTION

The nice thing about Fairbanks, my dad liked to joke, was that no matter what direction we took out of town, we soon arrived in Nowhere.

He meant the wilderness, the wild, the bush, untamed nature—whatever one called it, the very thing that had attracted him and others to the remote center of a vast territory bigger than all the U.S. western states put together.

Many rushed to Alaska's interior for gold, of course, with a dream of filling pokes with nuggets after a couple of summers and then sailing home to the "states"–or "Outside" as we called anyplace that wasn't Alaska—to lord it over the timid sods who had lingered behind.

Some arrived (and still do) to flee faraway troubles. Nobody much cared. Fairbanks became a place where you could restart your life. It was the end of the road for a long time.

Others, like my dad and mom, came for other reasons—he to work and hunt and fish and poke around the bush in his spare time, she with no choice in the matter, having arrived as a toddler born in Dawson, Yukon Territory, Canada, during the Klondike Gold Rush.

By the time I was born in 1934, Fairbanks remained remote—very remote.

To get to the states, we traveled 300 miles south on the Richardson Highway, a potholed lane barely the width of a sedan. The Richardson sported dust, mud, snow, and ice depending on the season. The road meandered through forests, over bare uplands, and across glaciered mountain passes on a spine-crunching drive to the tiny town of Valdez on saltwater. From there, Seattle's docks lay a week away.

Or we traveled on the Alaska Railroad to the slightly larger town of Anchorage, 365 miles to the southeast, and 105 miles beyond to Seward, another small saltwater settlement with passenger sailings to Seattle.

As a little boy, holding my dad's hand, I gazed up with amazement at the shiny Lockheed Lodestar that Pan American Airways landed at Weeks Field, the old Fairbanks ballpark that bush pilots had converted into an unpaved landing field with hangers. PAA touted this flight as the beginning of scheduled commercial air passenger service between Fairbanks and Seattle. World War II crimped that.

Aside from a handful of roadhouses, decaying mining camps, and Indian villages, Fairbanks provided most of the civilization, such as it was, for hundreds of miles in all directions.

It was a tiny, isolated town — a walk away from wilderness — where a boy could, and did, find an abundance of adventure.

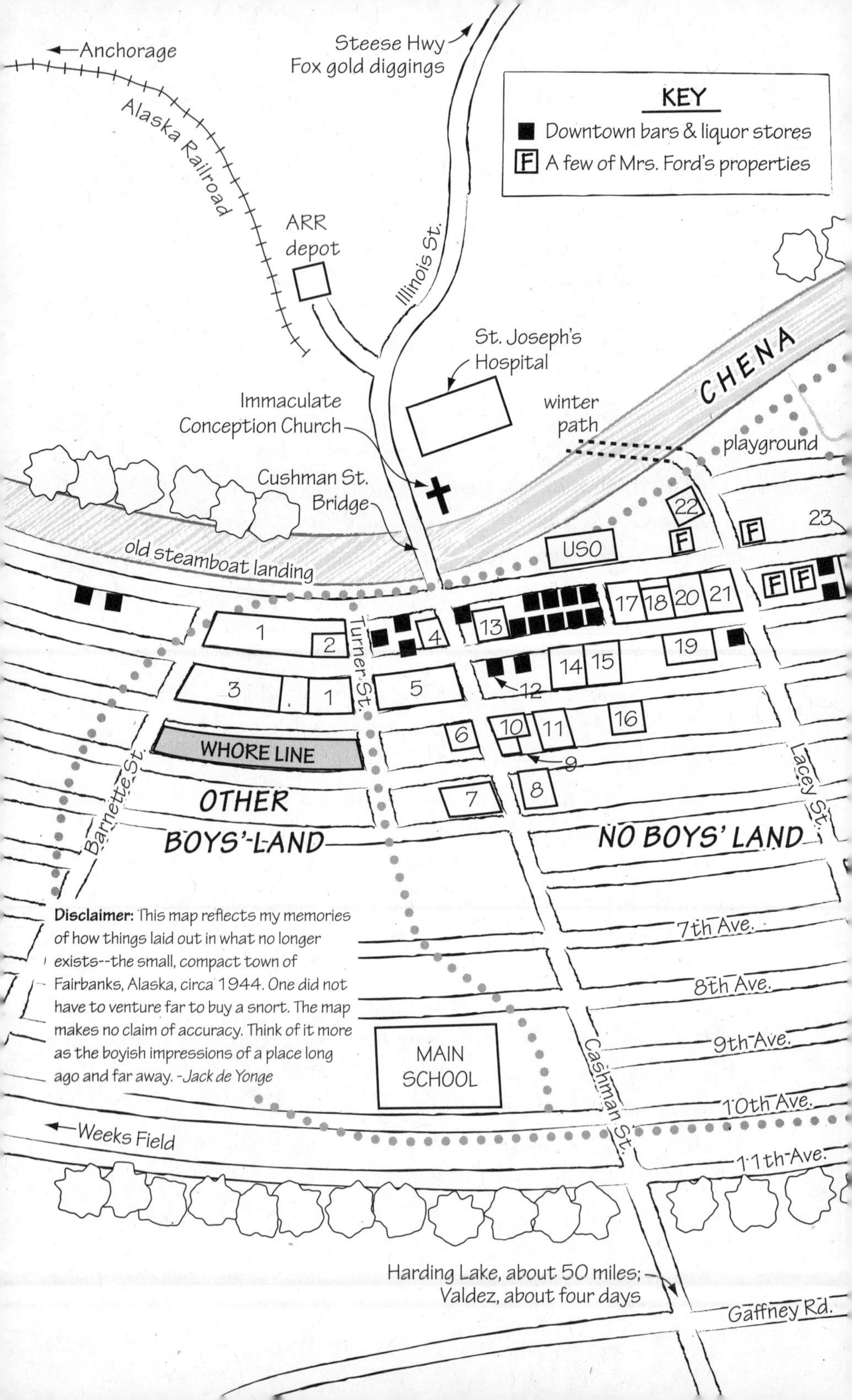
Anchorage
Steese Hwy
Fox gold diggings
KEY
Downtown bars & liquor stores
F A few of Mrs. Ford's properties
Alaska Railroad
ARR
depot
Illinois St.
St. Joseph's
Hospital
CHENA
Immaculate
Conception Church
winter
path
playground
Cushman St.
Bridge
22
23
USO
old steamboat landing
17
18
20
21
1
2
Turner St.
4
13
19
3
1
5
12
14
15
6
10
11
16
WHORE LINE
9
8
7
Barnette St.
OTHER
BOYS'-LAND
NO BOYS' LAND
Lacey St.
Disclaimer: This map reflects my memories of how things laid out in what no longer exists--the small, compact town of Fairbanks, Alaska, circa 1944. One did not have to venture far to buy a snort. The map makes no claim of accuracy. Think of it more as the boyish impressions of a place long ago and far away. -Jack de Yonge
7th Ave.
8th Ave.
9th Ave.
MAIN
SCHOOL
Cashman St.
10th Ave.
Weeks Field
11th Ave.
Harding Lake, about 50 miles;
Valdez, about four days
Gaffney Rd.

A boy's view of

FAIRBANKS, ALASKA

CIRCA 1944

RIVER
old steamboat landing
Graehl Landing
slough where Donny drowned
ballpark
HOMELAND
winter path
swimming pool
de Yonge Cabin
Wendell Ave.
1st Ave.
24
2nd Ave.
3rd Ave.
4th Ave.
5th Ave.
6th Ave.
7th Ave.
Dunkel St.
Hall St.
Noble St.
Clay St.
Clay St. Cemetery
Jacob's gardens
sawmill
military base
Ladd Field →

Downtown points of interest:

1. N.C. Store
2. N.C. Power Plant
3. N.C. Salmon Shed
4. 1st National Bank
5. Federal Building
6. Family Shoe Store
7. City Hall
8. Gordon's Store
9. Adler's Bookstore
10. Waechter Bros. Meats
11. Nerland's Furniture
12. Lavery's Grocery
13. Model Café
14. Empress Theater
15. Co-op Drugs
16. Jessen's Weekly
17. Piggly Wiggly's
18. Pioneer Cab
19. Nordale Hotel
20. News-Miner
21. Lacey St. Theater
22. Military Prophylactic Station
23. Bus Depot
24. Charlie Main's Store
25. Nick The Greek's Cabin
26. Mort Cass Warehouse
27. Case Home
28. Burnett home
29. Hatless Joe's Cabin
30. Heman home
31. Irwin home
32. Drouin home
33. Drouin Garage

One

EXPLOSIVE DAY ONE

I skidded into existence early the morning of July 4, 1934 in Fairbanks, Alaska, when a great "BOOM!" startled my mother into making a sudden contraction that shot me, forehead first, into the world.

A case of dynamite had exploded on a crude raft in the Chena River, a couple of hundred feet away from her bed in Saint Joseph's Hospital. Independence Day, then and for years after, was an anniversary wildly celebrated in this last of the north's gold-rush towns. Fairbanks was a dying hamlet of fewer than two thousand survivors, surrounded by the interior wilderness of a subcontinent one-fifth the size of the rest of the United States. Fairbanksans, as they called themselves, had to provide their own amusements. And every Fourth of July they did—with dynamite, acetylene gas, firecrackers big and small, rockets, parades, boat races, speeches, picnics, children's races, baseball games, an abundance of beer and whiskey, and a brawl or two. Men outnumbered women 2 to 1.

On this day, the celebrants hadn't intended to rouse the hospital patients and staff with the first dynamite blast of the holiday. They were more interested in startling friends partaking in the dark, dank, dingy, and smoky saloons across the river.

The power of my expulsion perhaps shaped my pate because a few minutes later, as fusillades of fireworks cracked and banged outside, my father, Harry de Yonge, strolled smiling into our hospital room where I contentedly sucked a nipple, gazed upon me as my mother looked up proudly, and exclaimed:

"He looks just like Jo-Jo the Pinheaded Boy!"

He was not predicting I might become a pointy-headed intellectual. His flash of recognition apparently confused the names of two famous circus-sideshow attractions of his youth and early manhood, Jo-Jo the Dog-faced Boy and Zip the Pinhead.

My mother, Eva Marie Delaney de Yonge, until that moment may have felt she was suckling the next best thing to the Baby Jesus, her first child differing from the holy carpenter only by begetter and method of conception. Hearing my father's words, she flared as only Irish can. Celtic neurons, wired from brain to spleen to tongue, fired.

In a moment of tranquil recollection years later over a noggin of gin and lemonade, my dad said Mom's eloquence expressing injury and outrage scorched him from toes to tonsure. An attending nun in the room, one of the Sisters of Providence who operated the frontier hospital, blanched and reached for her rosary beads, muttering a few beads' worth of prayer in hope of relieving my mother later of a few extra eons in Purgatory for her outburst.

My life thus commenced with a constant of my boyhood—a family row.

Dad soon retreated to the hospital's tiny waiting room, he said, for a cigar and a nip of recently legalized Old Crow from his hip flask. Better to drink it than eat it. He was two months from turning fifty-four.

Mom was thirty-three, born in Dawson, Yukon Territory, Canada, to Dan and Mary McDonough Delaney, stampeders in the Klondike Gold Rush. Both were pure lace-curtain Irish. Dan was born in Canada and Mary in Minnesota, each to parents who had fled to North America to escape Ireland's Great Potato Famine and English cruelty and misrule.

In her first years, Mother lived on or near Delaney diggings in the Klondike, moved to the gold-rush settlement of Fox, north of Fairbanks, and then settled with her family on the Delaney homestead east of Fairbanks. Throughout her twenties, before marrying my father, she lived and worked in San Francisco, where her folks and sister had ended up battered and near broke. Mom was black-haired, blue-eyed, buxom, smart, vivacious, hard-working indoors and out, superstitiously Catholic, and trigger-tempered. She could forgive a slight but never forget it or fail to mention it later.

My father was tall, broad-shouldered, handsome, and humorous, a hunter and fisherman who liked boon companions, Mark Twain, schnapps, cigars, and ragtime piano. His marriage four years earlier to Eva Delaney after decades of bachelorhood surprised his family, friends and, I came to believe, him too. But he was not one to go back on his word.

Dad arrived in Fairbanks not long after its founding as a gold-rush trading camp. He hailed from San Francisco. His father, Captain John de Yonge (de Jonge), a grandfather I never knew, came from a Dutch ship-owning and seafaring family in Emden, Germany. Captain John owned and skippered a clipper ship. He sailed it with hard discipline to ports in North and South America. As an adolescent, my dad sailed several times with him from San Francisco around Cape Horn to Havana,

New Orleans, New York, and Boston, earning a rating as an able-bodied seaman. Dad liked to tell yarns about hanging onto icy shrouds with bare toes and grabbing icicled ropes with numbed fingers while swaying a hundred feet out over Cape Horn's black waves curling fifty feet high causing the ship to lift, heel, and yaw.

His mother, a grandmother I never knew, Louisa Ruth de Yonge, a German immigrant, managed a large brood of offspring and a boarding house near San Francisco's Mission District with tact and wit—two traits quite necessary when Captain de Yonge stumped around home with a parrot on his shoulder, cigar in his mouth, and stein of beer in his hand. Apparently my grandfather had a milder temper than his parrot, which swore in several languages, but most often in Dutch, a tongue eloquent in profanity. The parrot loved to bite bent-over buttocks, especially the captain's.

At the hospital entrance a few days after the dynamite helped blast me into the world, Dad helped my mother, with me in her arms, into the family's four-door, gray-green 1932 Plymouth sedan. It sported, like many Alaska cars in those days of unpaved, rutted and chuck-holed streets and roads, an extra spare tire on a wheel chained and padlocked to the wheeled spare that rode on a mount attached to the trunk. The trunk stored extra tire inner-tubes, patches, glue, and changing tools, all of which received constant exercise. The Plymouth served the family until 1948.

Dad drove us out into the dust and gravel of the town's main drag, Cushman Street, turning left. The car soon banged and rattled up a long inclined plane of heavy lumber planks that rose to the deck of the only bridge over the Chena River in those days. Its steel frame, timbers, and boards crunched and wobbled as traffic crossed the river.

On the other end of the bridge, Dad drove the Plymouth down a steeper incline, turned left onto First Avenue or, as some called it, Front Street. The name you used depended on whether you were an old-timer who had been "in the country" for a long time or a cheechako—also known as a tenderfoot—fresh from the "Outside." Old-timers talked of Front Street. "Outside" referred to the continental United States, also known to this day as "the Lower 48"—a collection of places filled with softies who didn't understand or appreciate Alaska and the pure, rugged souls who ventured there.

By virtue of being born in Fairbanks, though only a few days old, already I qualified as a Sourdough. This was a rank of high standing in Interior Alaska. It still is.

The town Dad drove us through that summer morning, just eighteen months after Adolph Hitler achieved power, displayed to the wondering eye then and for years to come, streets of false-fronted commercial buildings, many of them bars, many of them closed for a decade or longer and slumping in decrepitude; and streets of small lumber-built "stick" or frame houses intermixed with many log cabins. Most cabins were tiny, easy to heat in the soul-numbing winters of the place. Many had sod roofs from which grass and fireweed sprouted. Because of the uneven melting of the permafrost on which they sat, some cabins were tilted and many cabins had sunk a couple of feet below ground level. Most sidewalks, where there were sidewalks, were lumber. In the summer, the quiet, narrow streets were muddy and puddled after a rainstorm, and dusty when dry. It was not so quiet in 1904 when my old man, then twenty-three, arrived. He found a boom settlement of tents, cabins of freshly hewed logs, and buildings erected with green lumber. Named after a U.S. senator who would become vice-president under Teddy Roosevelt, Fairbanks soon would boast in and around itself a population of ten thousand people and was growing. For a few years, it was the biggest city north of Vancouver, British Columbia.

When word got out in 1902 that gold had been found in the hills north of the Chena River, all kinds of men, women, and children rushed to the area. They arrived by paddle-wheeler steamboats and on foot and horseback, many from the Klondike and Dawson, where most folks never found the easy gold. In just a few years, Dawson had changed from importing champagne from France to exporting disappointed hoards that had expected to pick gold off the streets but had found only horse turds there. Fairbanks, accessible by water, offered a renewed prayer that grubbing for gold in the nearby creeks would fill their pokes.

Also rushing to Fairbanks by riverboats were those who had stampeded a couple of years earlier from the Klondike and elsewhere to Nome, on a desolate shore of the Bering Sea several hundred miles west of Fairbanks. Some scored big by extracting gold from the sand of Nome's beaches, but the beaches had played out in a hurry. Those with big money, big machinery, big political clout, and little honesty exploited the real diggings on shore—the new arrivals. The disappointed or cheated rushed on to Fairbanks and the nearby placer creeks for another roll of the dice. Not for nothing did many a mining operation around Fairbanks call itself Last Hope or Last Chance.

My dad arrived in Fairbanks looking not for gold but to take a job as a hardwareman at the large new mercantile operation, the Northern Commercial Company, or N.C. as it was known, a major force during the town's first half-century.

Headquartered in Seattle, the N.C. established itself on First Avenue in 1903 and built a big store that sold everything—hardware, groceries, booze, furniture, clothing, diamonds and rubies, office supplies, and furs. You name it, the N.C. probably had it. The N.C. power plant supplied electricity, steam, and foul air to all who wanted it and to some who didn't. The N.C. sold cars, trucks, and tractors. It ran the telephone company. It supplied bales of smoked dog salmon for the town's thousands of sled dogs that for decades howled a wondrous serenade whenever the N.C. power plant's steam whistle blew.

The N.C. sold gasoline at the pump, in cans, and in barrels. It sold dynamite, good for many things including waking the town up on the Fourth of July. It serviced dozens of smaller N.C. stores in tiny Native villages and mining settlements across the vast Alaska territory. People joked that it even sold sex. Fairbanks' other main commercial enterprise, a red-light district consisting of a block of log-cabin cribs on Fourth Avenue, butted against N.C. property. The Line, or Whore Line as it was called, operated in the middle of Fairbanks for a half-century.

Dad had disliked being a sailor on windjammers. He had tried carrying hod, digging ditches, selling typewriters door to door, picking hops, boot-legging, and trapping skunks and carting them alive for sale to street markets in San Francisco's Chinatown. Selling skunks was an occupation, he confided to me, which held small promise of social success. He got a job at San Francisco Hardware. He was good at it. He had something a hardwareman needs, a phenomenal memory.

Later, he moved to Seattle Hardware on Seattle's Skid Road. There, he heard about an N.C. hardware job in the new burg of Fairbanks. He signed up, booked passage on a coastal steamship, disembarked at Valdez, and spent a week on the Richardson Trail on horseback with other pilgrims heading north.

That day we left the hospital, Dad drove Mom and me, Johnny (I was always Johnny to him), to the family cabin on Wendell Avenue. He steered the Plymouth past the abodes of "boys" of the kind who whooped it up in the Malemute and other saloons when they had money. Some of these he suspected of blowing up that case of dynamite fateful in my launching.

One was Elam "Burning Daylight" Harnish, who in his youth was the most famous dog musher and racer on the Yukon. He inspired the fictional hero of Jack London's 1910 best-selling potboiler novel, *Burning Daylight.* Now, in his declining years,

Harnish lived in a Wendell Avenue log cabin. It sat among a clutch of other log cabins sheltering single men in a big stand of Cottonwood trees. Harnish got his nickname by rising early and waking everyone else by hollering, "Get up, get up! You're burning daylight!"

Burning Daylight's skin and eyes reflected little exposure to sunshine but considerable exposure to moonshine when I used to talk to him as a kid who delivered his paper. He was a good tipper.

Another set of boys lived across the street in a two-story log house that tilted to one side. There resided Nick the Greek, Nick Nicodemus, and his band of merry woodcutters, four or five or ten of them, depending. They supplied logs of white spruce to the lumber mill for food money; for drinking money, they sold split spruce and birch firewood to homes all over town. They all looked as if they drank more than they ate.

A block onward, the Plymouth rolled by the lash-up of Charlie Cook, who lived in a peeled log cabin with a dozen or so Indians.

In his riverboat one day, Charlie had held a second too long onto a stick of capped dynamite with a sputtering fuse. He turned to fling the stick into a pool where king salmon rolled. The blast was intended to levitate them to the surface, stunned for gaffing. The dynamite flew from his hand but not far enough, nor fast enough. From what remained of Charlie's pureed paw, Fairbanks docs fused a flexible flap. Once his pals saw it, they gave Charlie a nickname—"Catcher's Mitt."

Likely it was Charlie and his pals in Charlie's boat who pulled the raft carrying the case of dynamite, lit a fused stick, and rowed like hell away to keep their heads from becoming like Charlie's paw.

Flash! Bang! And that's how I came to be born on the Fourth of July.

Two
LITTLE EVA

In the summer of 1904, after a journey from Dawson down the Yukon River and up its tributary, the Tanana River, my grandma, Mary Delaney, and her son Finian, seven, and daughter Eva, three, walked off a sternwheeler at the town of Chena at the mouth of the Chena River, a few miles west of Fairbanks.

Grandma shouldered a pack, took her children's hands, and started a two-day trek across muskeg in the company of other pilgrims heading for Fox on Goldstream, which, with other creeks in the Fairbanks Mining District, came to yield more gold than the Klondike.

My mom remembered that hike as a hot, humid torture of mosquitoes, moose flies, black flies, and gnats, and as a jostle of testy adults and crying children. No insect repellent that worked longer than a few minutes existed in those days. You suffered the bugs and endured.

Mom's dad, Dan Delaney, and his partner, Jimmy Lang, another Irishman, awaited them near Fox.

In 1898, before my mother was born, the Delaneys and Lang had survived Soapy Smith and his bandits in Skagway and then had climbed Chilkoot Pass in rainstorms and clouds of bugs, with Mary grasping little Finian by the hand. The men had to make several trips from tidewater to the summit where they piled all their gear and valuables to prove to a detachment of the Royal Canadian Mounted Police at the Canadian border that, along with money, they had sufficient gear and enough rice and beans to survive a year in the Klondike wilderness.

After weeks of toil and adventure, during which Delaney and Lang earned extra money by guiding other parties through a dangerous rapids on the upper Yukon River, they arrived to join other stampeders jamming Dawson's rough streets. Like the rest, Delaney and Lang hurried to make claims along creeks yet unstaked. Like most stampeders, they mucked and moiled for four years, finding enough gold to keep them in oatmeal and under a roof but not much else. My mother was born in Dawson in 1900.

Two years later, news of a gold strike in Central Alaska galvanized the family. Delaney and Lang took off. Mary and my mom and Finian hunkered down in a cabin in Dawson awaiting a summons to head downriver.

Our family stories don't make clear whether Delaney and Lang snowshoed one hundred miles down the Yukon to Circle, carrying packs or dragging a sled; or whether they mushed there with dogs pulling a sled; or whether, as soon as the ice went out, they traveled by riverboat down the big river to Circle, a long-established mining camp with bars, a theater, and a fancy whore house.

After breakup, the gold-seekers flooded out of Circle for the new bonanza north of the Chena. Those with gold bought passage on riverboats to Chena, by way of the Tanana River, and hiked to Fox. Others stayed onboard, getting off in Fairbanks, at first known as Barnette's Cache, a burgeoning tent town. E.T. Barnette had set up a trading post the summer before. He was an affable rogue with a taste for celebrity status, for other men's wives, and for other people's money. He greeted newcomers with whiskey and other necessities, charging gold-rush prices. (Barnette eventually looted the town's bank and ran off to Hollywood.)

From Barnette's camp, well-trodden trails led men and horses to where hundreds of prospectors were ripping up the countryside in their frantic scramble for gold. That was the easy route to the new bonanza.

Delaney and Lang instead humped it on foot from Circle to conserve their cash and gold, knowing they would need money to establish a placer-mining operation if they found gold. Many an old prospector told yarns about this Klondike miner or that who had panned enough gold to know he had great prospects, but did not have enough dollars to develop the mine, forcing him to sell his claim, or a share of it, to strangers. Those with the most gold in their pokes took the biggest share.

My grandfather and Lang lugged shoulder-biting canvas packs. To these they lashed shovels, picks, pots, and pans. They followed rough trails running southwest into the Yukon foothills and then down to the Birch Creek flats. Living on beans and bacon, they slogged through the barren hills and domes between Circle and the new bonanza. They climbed high above the timber line into caribou country, and then dropped down into the valley of the Chatanika River. The known gold strikes were in the next watershed south.

This sounds easy enough, unless one has hiked Interior Alaska during the summer when mosquitoes run a million to the square meter. Moose flies, with jaws that can pinch through moose hide, evoke exquisite delights on the human hide. Black flies, small and fast, drill your skin by the dozen. Swarms of gnats (no-see-'ems) attack by the hundreds. Nothing amuses more than to realize that gnat bites are swelling your eyes shut.

Add to these pleasures the sensual gratifications of hiking with a bent, aching back on slippery tussocks surrounded by a foot or two of water—tussocks that bowed under your weight so that your boot slipped and jammed down into sulfurous, black muck that sucked the boot off your foot. Add to this the pleasures of fording cold, rushing creeks on large, round rocks slick with algae, then tumbling backwards, to land upside down, with your pack holding you under water while your legs thrashed for traction.

Dan Delaney and Jimmy Lang, like the other prospectors, breakfasted on hope and dined on desperation. Both sustained them. They finished the trek in good stead. This testifies to their physical condition. Delaney was thirty-nine, Lang about the same. By fall, they had claims staked well upstream of Discovery Claim on Gilmore Creek.

The Fairbanks Gold Rush is associated with domes—great rounded hills vented from volcanic fissures a million years ago.

The gold discovered by Felix Pedro and Tom Gilmore originated from veins of gold that flowed up in the magma of the domes. Over geologic time, some of the gold was eroded to the surface by gravity, wind, ice, and water. Water pushed gold dust, flakes, and nuggets downhill. They lodged in stream-bottom gravels that yielded the placer gold—gold in place—that was panned by squatting prospectors.

Experience taught miners that other gold deposits existed deep under their feet—placer gold deposited eons ago in old creek beds long covered with thick soil, usually muskeg, and perpetually frozen as permafrost. This gold they reached by tunneling sometimes hundreds of feet down to the old creek beds. Windlasses and other apparatus hoisted paydirt to the surface. Miners flumed the paydirt over wooden or metal riffles that trapped the heavy gold for hand-picking and panning. Fine dust they sopped up in mercury. Then in a still, they evaporated and retrieved the costly mercury for re-use. The retort's residue contained the gold. If the miners inhaled the mercury's vapors, eventually the mercury would eat away enough brain cells to madden them, to cause Mad Hatters disease or give them the shakes, a form of Parkinson's disease. Old Fairbanks hotels harbored grizzled miners who shook and shuddered from having sniffed too much mercury and, even in December, waved away imaginary mosquitoes in the lobby.

Delaney and Lang sank a shaft to bedrock, and then they "drifted" it laterally from side to side, to follow meandering veins of gold. They built a cabin and sheds, cut lumber, and constructed platforms, flumes and derricks.

The simplest mine required grinding labor with hand tools to dig a shaft and shore it. You grubbed paydirt while you knelt in a drift tunnel fifty or more feet underground, barely high enough to accommodate your spine. Your candle flickered in an atmosphere poor with oxygen and rich with carbon dioxide. The prospect of death from cave-in or suffocation salted your digging with anxiety. You wrestled fears that your partner might stop hand-pumping air to you or that he might cower from risking his own life to save yours if, at a set interval, you failed to tug a signal line.

My grandfather and Lang wintered on their claim, my mother said. By letter, Delaney told my grandma to move the family from Dawson to the mine.

Delaney met his family at Fox, where he had built a tiny log cabin for them. There, he alternated between hiring out as a carpenter and working with Lang at the mine. The Delaneys stayed in Fox for four years. The camp's population swelled from a few Indians to several thousand stampeders. A year later, a new narrow-gauge railroad chuffed from Fairbanks to Fox, Pedro Camp, Gilmore, and other nearby mining villages (all long gone). Now, you could ride the train into Fairbanks for supplies and be back the same day. Fox boasted its own local necessities—a brothel, bars, hotel, general store, blacksmith, machine shop, and grammar school.

Within a decade, Fox became another dying town. Easy gold played out. Profits depended on investing big money in heavy machinery. The need to bring in such machinery helped drive the completion of the Alaska Railroad from Seward to Fairbanks in 1923.

By then, Goldstream and nearby diggings had attracted Guggenheim's U.S. Smelting, Refining and Mining Company of Massachusetts, under various corporate guises one of the great, ravenous, rapacious mining combines of North America and later the world.

The company started Fairbanks Exploration Company, also known as the F.E. Company, and purchased hundreds of claims around Fox. With cheap labor, it installed large dredges that chewed up the creeks. Great profits flowed. The dredges devoured settlements in the way, including most of Fox, turning them into high, serried piles of sterile, pastel rocks called tailing piles. By the 1940s, all that remained of Fox was a general store where a few old boys gathered daily around a pot-bellied wood stove to swap tales of old glories.

In 1907, my grandpa fell down a mine shaft and broke his back, my mother said. He was a tough bird. Given the crude state of medicine then, it was a miracle that he survived the ministrations of area doctors. But he could mine no longer. He and Lang sold out their operation for a fraction of what they thought it was worth but were happy to get that, Mom said.

While Delaney recuperated in a rented log cabin in Fairbanks, my grandma took in sewing and fashioned women's hats for sale. Eventually he began working again as a carpenter and farmer. The Delaneys homesteaded land across the Chena River a little upstream of Fairbanks on a tongue of land called Bentley Island, formed on one of the big S-bends on the river. Noyes Slough separated it from the mainland. Jimmy Lang claimed land on the mainland farther upriver where he gardened, trapped, and cut firewood. He fiddled for pay at saloons and parties evenings and weekends.

In the summer, the Delaneys on Bentley Island were a far piece from the services of downtown Fairbanks. They reached town by boat, or on foot or on horseback along the Chena's north bank, crossing sloughs on swinging bridges to reach the Cushman Street Bridge. The trip into town became easier after freeze-up when they and others used a myriad of paths across the ice for hiking to various parts of the community. My mother, her brother, and later a sister, Marguerite, born in 1911, walked several miles directly to school once the Chena froze.

The whole family spent a long Sunday walking to and from town to attend mass at the Church of the Immaculate Conception next to Saint Joseph's Hospital.

On the homestead, my grandfather built a sizeable log house and stable from white spruce. He bought a horse for clearing, plowing, and fetching supplies.

The short Fairbanks growing season is intense. The first of June is considered the traditional first frost-free day you can rely on for planting. The days then and for the next ninety days supply long hours of sunlight, direct or radiant, granted that Interior Alaska's summers can be cloudy and wet.

Settlers found they could grow truck vegetables of surprising excellence and size. Because the early mining civilization depended on horses, they also planted barley and oats. Sometimes the harvest yielded enough to feed livestock through the winter; but then, sometimes it did not, especially if there was an early freeze in late August. During what pioneer

Fairbanksans called the Early Days, many a family dobbin ended up as January's pot roast.

A ready market existed in town and at the mines for vegetables and fodder. Long summer days permitted my grandfather to tend his crops early in the morning and late into the evenings, allowing him to earn carpenter's wages during the day. My grandmother and Finian, and later my mother, sold garden strawberries and raspberries door to door.

They also picked and sold wild raspberries, strawberries (tiny, tart, and delicious), currants, low-bush cranberries (lingonberries), high-bush cranberries, which perfumed birch forests in the fall, and blueberries. Blueberries grew in patches so abundant that women and children could pick them while ignoring the black bears (but not the grizzlies) that stuffed paws full of berries, leaves, and twigs into their maws. In late summer and early fall, my mother and Finian carried five-gallon buckets of blueberries with shoulder yokes into Fairbanks to sell to the Model Café and other restaurants.

The Delaneys appeared to thrive before America's 1917 entry into the First World War. They sent Finian to Minnesota in his teens to attend a Catholic college. Attending college was a rarity then. He mailed a picture postcard of himself home to "Mary Delaney, Fairbanks, Alaska," such being enough to ensure delivery. He was handsome and smiling in a pressed suit, shirt, tie, and cap. The writing, hard to decipher, reports his team beat Saint Joseph's College in baseball, 48-0, a debacle for Saint Joe's.

Finian, who registered for the draft the same day as my father, disappeared in, around, or from Fairbanks in 1917. He had received his draft notice, my mother said, and walked away from the Bentley Island homestead one morning with a valise, on orders to join other draftees for transport by primitive bus from Fairbanks south to the saltwater port of Valdez, a tedious journey of many days on the rutted, potholed, graveled Richardson Highway, successor to the old Richardson

Trail. The Richardson traversed wide muskeg flats when it was not winding into, through, and out of the Alaska Range, where glacial torrents raged through scenery magnificent to the eye but difficult and dangerous and wearing to the body and soul. The buses stopped at roadhouses to feed and bed passengers. The drive from Fairbanks to Valdez took four days, often longer, depending on road conditions, which were never good.

Finian never made it to the draftees' mustering point that morning, my mom said. Late in the day, Army authorities came looking for him. He was not the only young man who had failed to report. The family sweated. By evening my grandfather had organized a large search. But Finian had vanished. Months later, my mother said, berry-pickers found a skeleton in the woods on Bentley Island. Authorities never identified it. The Delaneys, including my mother to her dying day, believed that a neighbor had murdered Finian, a neighbor with whom Dan Delaney had feuded over a piece of land. Finian's disappearance, my mother said, wilted my grandmother forever after.

However, a single paragraph appearing in a short-lived Fairbanks newspaper of the day reported that Finian Delaney had disappeared at the Gulkana Roadhouse, where the party of draftees had stopped one night. The paragraph speculated that Finian had deserted at a place where a long-established trail headed toward the Klondike. It also speculated Finian had been murdered. It left it at that.

I like to think that as a good Irish-American lad, Finian deserted. The Delaneys, like many North American Irish, sentimentalized an Ireland they had never seen. Ireland in 1917 was in armed, bloody rebellion against the English. Going to war to save the hides of the bastardly, cruel, oppressing British soured Irish-American lads. It comforts to think that somewhere in North America lives a tribe of Delaneys, although perhaps not named such, sired by Uncle Finian, who was brave enough to run for it when he could.

In 1918, my mother graduated from Fairbanks High School. She was a handsome maiden with long black hair, bright blue eyes, and a well-developed bust and rear, all riding with modest sway over small feet under trim ankles. In a town with far more men than women, she captured attention. I know that my father noticed her.

I say this because ten years later, in the summer of 1928, on Market Street in San Francisco, my mother was standing before a window at Weinstein's department store when she saw the reflection of a tall, good-looking man in a three-piece brown suit and fedora walk up behind her and say:

"Hello, Fairbanks."

Not much of a pickup line, but it worked.

My mother's parents had migrated from Fairbanks to Phoenix in 1920 because her sister Marguerite, then nine, suffered agonizing, deforming rheumatoid arthritis. At that time, doctors could do even less than doctors today (and that's not much) to relieve this relentless immunological disease in which one's own antibodies attack one's nerves and bones and tendons, swelling and twisting the joints. A chief prescription for dealing with arthritis of any kind, and still as good as it was when it helped the first cave people, is to go where it's hot and dry. Central Alaska is not that place.

The Delaneys headed for Phoenix, then a small town in a sea of sand and cacti. My mother stayed behind in Fairbanks where she worked as a secretary, her first real job. She lived in a rooming house for young maidens.

Baking in the Arizona desert in the days before air-conditioning did not help Marguerite—known forever, in my mother's parlance, as "poor" Marguerite. My grandparents moved Marguerite to San Francisco. Why, I know not. It certainly offered little dryness and warmth. My mom joined them. They rented a dark, chilly flat at 326 Waller Street, one block south and east of the intersection of Fillmore and Haight. Dan, Mary, and Marguerite lived there the rest of their lives.

In the 1920s, my mom worked as a typist and stenographer at the Shell Oil Company office on Market Street, a job she held when my father came up behind her to utter those immortal words in our family: "Hello, Fairbanks."

I have no idea what the Delaneys lived on. Only my mother worked. I know that in San Francisco the Delaneys scraped by. Even so, shortly after my mother ran away to marry my father, there was money enough for Marguerite to commute to the University of California at Berkeley. Her journey to school found her most days a week hobbling with crutches over to Fillmore to catch the streetcar that would take her to the terminal for the ferry to Oakland across the bay, and from there by street car to the great campus. She had been a good pianist until her fingers twisted. She wanted to be a composer, but arthritis defeated her education. It stranded her, except for special taxi and ambulance rides to doctors, at 326 Waller Street and its gloom for the next forty years.

After my grandparents died, Marguerite lived there alone, taking communion from visiting priests and tended by visiting nurses, other help, and sometimes my mother. Meanwhile, the neighborhood turned. By the late 1950s, Haight-Fillmore became a haven for poor blacks. By the late 1960s, it metamorphosed again under a cloud of incense and pot smoke into a Mecca for hippies. In the late 1970s, the wine-and-cheese crowd gentrified it. It was and is a long way from Fox and gold-rush Fairbanks.

Three

BABY JACK

The de Yonge family mansion stood at 117 Wendell Avenue in the last block before Wendell sloped down to the shore of the Chena River through a forest of willows. These trees grew along the Chena all the way downriver to the center of Fairbanks and then again on the other side of the town. The willows were enticing. Winos camped in them. Lovers canoodled there. Boys frolicked in them, built forts there, warred, and declared armistices to sneak barefooted to watch the amorous of all persuasions explore and occupy sundry orifices. For Fairbanks lads, the willows provided sex educations that would not become legal until decades later.

Our house was among the smallest of five on the block. The smallest was another log cabin where Clay Street ran into Wendell. It had a decrepit roof that sprouted fireweed and onions in season. It had sunk nearly out of sight by the time my father drove my mother and me, Baby Pinhead, home from the hospital. Everyone knew that Jack London had lived here. It gave no small pleasure to show the cabin to visitors from Outside. Never mind that Jack London never had been to Fairbanks. His loss, everyone said.

Our cabin, which I was to occupy for the next sixteen years, carried no such literary distinction, nor for that matter any distinction in architecture.

Whoever built our cabin had followed a common gold-rush technique. I say "whoever" because although my mother insisted that Grandpa Delaney built it, the timing conflicts with Grandpa's prospecting and mining out on the creeks to the north. It was a subject upon which my father was mum. The builder dug a twenty- by twenty-five-foot hole about six feet deep in the thick, gray silt deposited almost every spring and sometimes in the summer when the Chena River flooded. The hole served as cellar. The builder used spruce logs about two feet in diameter, planing them flat top and bottom, and laid them along and back from the edges of the hole. These served as the foundation and, given the inherently temporary status of a gold rush, they weren't expected to hold up forever. In the early days, the aim was to get a roof over your head before winter. If you couldn't do that, there would be no future, no chance to get rich picking up nuggets out of creeks.

The walls he built of logs, round on the outside but planed flat on the inside. Beams and roof runners were squared logs and poles. The roof he pitched steeply because of the heavy snows. He roofed it with small boards. All lumber in those early days came from local white spruce. On top of the roof boards, he layered sod about eighteen inches deep, replete with live grasses and wild flowers. By the time my folks bought the cabin, sheets of rusting steel ("tin," in the local slang) had replaced the sod. This was upscale roofing, real commercial sheets, sold where my dad worked, at the N.C. By the time I was old enough to notice such things, I saw that many cabins had rusting roofs covered with cut and flattened five-gallon gasoline cans emblazoned with Standard Oil or Mobile Oil logos.

Inside, the builder covered the log walls with rough-hewn boards. Outside, he chinked the spaces between the logs with moss, mud or oakum—whatever was handy. Then he covered the chinks with thick, white putty, which soon would crack and let in frigid air. Every summer, my dad replaced cracking putty. The putty gave the cabin white horizontal stripes and a festive air.

Inside, between the outer and inner walls, the builder stuffed shredded newspapers for insulation, a common practice of the day. Shredded newspapers made cheap insulation, wonderful nesting for rats, and excellent tinder for the frequent fires that burned Fairbanks cabins to the ground, especially on the coldest winter days when inhabitants allowed wood fires to burn too hot, risking a chimney fire.

The original cabin had no storm porches. The street door swung into the front room. This living room was twenty-five feet across and ten feet deep. It had two windows facing north toward Wendell Avenue and a small, high window looking west. On the left as you came in from the street, a door led to the only bedroom, a ten- by ten-foot square where my parents slept. The bedroom had a large window facing south, overlooking our large backyard.

Inside the front room, a door to the right opened into the kitchen, an area fifteen feet wide and ten feet deep. In the kitchen loomed a large white and black enamel wood range, which gulped armloads of birch, aspen, and spruce and at first supplied the only heat in the cabin. Beside the stove jutted a zinc sink, with a red hand pump, later to be replaced with an electric pump and taps for hot and cold water. But in those early days you primed the hand pump with water stored in a jug for that purpose. After a half-dozen gurgling strokes of the pump's cast-iron handle, out belched the brownish, sulphurous, iron-laden water for which Fairbanks is acclaimed.

On the floor before the sink lay a trap door, opened by a brass ring nestled in a cavity carved into the door's spruce boards. Lifted up and latched to the wall for safety's sake, the door revealed a lumber stairway descending into the dark dirt cellar, where, when I was about seven, Dad installed a wood furnace that he later converted to coal. The cellar was always cool. My folks used it not just to store trunks and the like, but also to cool and preserve vegetables and meat.

Across the kitchen from the sink, high narrow windows looked west into a neighbor's yard. Under the windows, a table, usually covered with a checkered oil cloth, accommodated four chairs. The kitchen also had cupboards for china and open shelves for pots and pans. White wallpaper embossed with blue fleurs-de-lis covered the walls. On the window sill my mom kept a large, metal alarm clock, always set ahead fifteen minutes for reasons she refused to explain. We de Yonges always dined in the future.

The back door and stairs off the kitchen led out into the large backyard, where a two-hole wooden outhouse sat slung over a cesspool that my dad dug with a shovel. For the first four years of my life, this privy served us summer and winter. In winter, we also used chamber pots that my folks lugged outdoors in the morning to dump into the privy.

Once, when we all had the flu, the chamber pots couldn't keep up. I was hauled outside and held upright on one of the frosted seats. This was a memorable occasion. It was forty to fifty below, when one exposes a bare rump to the frigid air only under great duress.

A large, cobwebbed shed stood behind the cabin. Among other things it held a walled-in but inoperative privy that during all the summers of my youth emitted smells of poops of yore.

Nearly eight years passed before my dad could afford to build a room about the size of the kitchen connecting the shed to the house. In the new room, he plumbed a flush toilet and a metal shower stall and built a large clothes closet.

Gray wallpaper covered the front room and bedroom walls. Entering from Wendell Avenue, you saw yourself in a mirror across the room, later partly blocked by a bookcase showcasing the voluminous World Book Encyclopedia. Next to the kitchen door sat my father's stuffed chair. Across from it, by the street window, sat a radio on a table. Between the windows and door was the rocking chair my mother loved. On the far end of the room, next to the bedroom door, resided a couch that my mother converted into a bed every night for me and, later, for me and my brother, Buzz.

The cabin was cozy, for comfort's sake and for ease of heating in extreme winters.

Decades later, I discovered cabins just like it in Russia. The savage Russian winters and taiga forests dictated similar results. Indeed, some historians say the classic log cabins of Alaska resembled the cabins Americans found in Alaska after the United States bought the vast region from Russia in 1867, a transaction in which the Russian government bribed enough U.S. senators to ensure that the purchase treaty would be ratified.

No phone ever jangled the atmosphere of the de Yonge cabin on Wendell Avenue. On my father's salary as a hardware clerk, we couldn't afford one, even when my mother worked as a secretary. We relied on the generosity of neighbors to make phone calls under the pressures of necessity. During my Fairbanks boyhood, the U.S. mail was delivered only to postal boxes in the downtown Federal Building. For many years, the only numbers I needed to remember were my age, birth date, grade in school, street address, and our post office box. (What mercies civilization today has brought us, requiring great lists of secret numbers to create our identities and requiring us to hide these numbers under passwords frequently forgotten.)

For the years I lived in the cabin, we depended on our four-door Plymouth sedan with gray cloth seats. In summers, Dad parked it in the gravel driveway between our cabin and the frame house next door. In winter, he parked it on our small front lawn where he could reach it with an electric cord to plug into its head-bolt heater, a necessity then as now in Fairbanks to keep engine oil viscous for starting at sub-zero temperatures.

My parents entertained frequently in our cabin. Neighbors dropped in without asking. It was expected. Bill Hunter, Jess Rust, Lou Joy, and other of Dad's N.C. colleagues often came by after work for what was called a "booster" of gin before going home. Dinner parties were set up in the living room, where my dad, after a few boosters, might take to our new piano to belt out ragtime and accompany sing-alongs.

The cabin, especially in winter's confines, pressure-cooked the fights my mother and father had. These usually were started by my mother with her terrier's temper and ended by my father who, not having said a word from start to finish, put on his boots and parka and fur hat and elbow mittens, and stomped out. He called it "letting her cool down," the same words he used when our Plymouth boiled over.

Four

EARTHQUAKE

CRASH! The whole house shook. Startled, I looked up from my oatmeal just as cupboard doors flew open and dishes and glasses cascaded onto my mother. My dad grabbed my shirt, lifting me up as my mother, wide-eyed, struggled to get up. "Watch out!" she warned. "The stove!"

Clutched under my dad's arm, I saw a big white kettle slide across the black top of the wood stove. Dad leaped for the door into the shed. Mom hollered again. The kettle slammed onto the floor, sloshing red berries and juice over the linoleum, just as Mom managed to get out the door behind us.

Outdoors in the sunshine, the earth rolled up and down. Dad pushed Mom toward the driveway. The birds had stopped singing. The Plymouth sedan rolled back and forth.

"Grab him, Eva!" Mom, braced against the heaving shed, pulled me against her.

Dad ran to the car, opened the driver's door, jumped on the running board, and dived inside head first. Over the rumbling of the earth I heard the screech of the emergency brake. The car stopped. The earth stopped. The Irwins next door piled out of their back door. Mom put me down, still holding on to my suspender.

"Earthquake!" Mr. Irwin said.

"Big goddamned thing," said my father. Donny Irwin, the boy next door, stood mute, puzzled.

I trailed my mom inside. She paused at the kitchen door. Hot, sweet cranberry juice covered the floor. "Oh, Lord," she muttered. Broken glass glinted in the red sea. The juice smelled wonderful.

"Go outside to your father," she ordered. Outside, the robins chortled again. The swallows in the three big boxes under the eves flitted again and twittered.

A week later, we drove down the trail—that's what Mom and Dad still called the Richardson—to look at the telegraph line and the ACS station. The telegraph line had been strung on spruce tripods by the ACS boys, as Dad called members of the U.S. Army Signal Corps who worked as the Alaska Communications System. At 40 Mile, we joined other people gawking at the two-story log ACS station, which leaned to one side and looked like a layer cake that someone had shaken.

We went on to the Salcha River and had a picnic. Dad fished. Mosquitoes swarmed. I know now that the Fairbanks earthquake of July 22, 1937, registering 7.3 on the Richter scale, was one of the most powerful quakes ever recorded in the United States and its possessions. Nobody was killed, but much booze from bottles that crashed to the floor in local liquor stores poured into the dirt streets. It was sorely missed.

Five

MY DISAPPOINTING NEW BROTHER

About the time of the earthquake, my dad sat in his living-room easy chair with me on his lap and my mother sitting on the arm. I had just turned three. He and Mom announced that soon I would have a baby brother or sister.

"I want a nigger baby!" I replied in a statement that instantly became part of our family lore.

How I learned this word I'm not sure. Though my parents shared racial prejudices of their time, neither used the word "nigger" except in the phrase "nigger in the woodpile." The phrase puzzled me for years as a child. Everyone had woodpiles but black people were not seen in Fairbanks until the Second World War, and then rarely.

My folks laughed at my request and said sure, and talked about what I had said, especially to visitors. Such talk convinced me I would have a black baby to play with.

As my mother swelled, my anticipation swelled with her. One morning near Christmas, Mom went away with Dad. Mrs. Korbo, the Finnish lady who lived catty-corner in a cabin across the street, took me to her house to wait. There, I indulged myself with her delicious almond cookies. That night, she took me back home, where she had kept the fire going, put me to bed on the couch, and lay down beside me.

The next day, Mom and Dad returned home with a swaddled object they deposited in the crib I once had occupied. Dad held me up so that I could peer into the crib. My eyes took in a disgusting sight—a pink, wrinkled creature that in no way fit my vision of a black baby. I howled in outrage. For the first time in my life, I tasted the bitterness of betrayal. Right or wrong, from that moment on, hug me and comfort me as they might, my parents had lost my trust and never fully regained it.

Eventually, I reconciled to the interloper, who turned out to be my brother, Harry Joseph, more commonly known as Buzz. He was born December 16, 1937.

A few days later, Santa Claus rattled down our stovepipe, popped (I supposed) out of the kitchen stove (I supposed), and deposited under the Christmas tree for me a large black Kewpie doll. For several days, I manipulated the doll as the glow of opening Christmas presents faded, visitors came and went, including my godfather Jimmy Lang, and glasses clinked and laughter stirred at the tale of my wanting a nigger baby. Now I had one. Its eyeballs rolled up and down or back and forth depending on how you moved the doll's head. I twisted its swiveled head, I lifted its arms, and I exercised its legs. I lifted its dress to peek at what equipment it had between its legs (none), an action that never failed to stir my mother to correct me if she saw me doing it in the presence of company, thus evoking more laughter. For the first time, I experienced the sting of embarrassment, being the object of merriment.

One day, I picked up the doll by the ankle and smashed its face against the side of the bookcase. That produced a most satisfying feeling. As the doll's face shattered, it revealed the whiteness of the material under the black paint. It was a phony. So I gave it another whack.

My mother yanked me up by the ear and satisfied herself by giving me several hard smacks on the ass that, in the custom of the day, I richly deserved. Tantrums were not allowed, Freudian outbursts were neither recognized nor tolerated, and breaking things bought with good money was punished.

I yowled in pain, stimulating my mother to smack me harder and faster with a ferocity that today no doubt would amount to felonious assault. My shrieks that day did not carry to the minions of law and order, however, and it wouldn't have done any good if they did. Whupping kids was looked upon as hard, tedious work necessary to bend rebellious little souls toward righteousness.

Who knows? That spanking and countless others Mom applied to my heinie may account for my saintliness today.

Six

WILL ROGERS, WILEY POST, AND ME

For years, our family photograph album was adorned by a black and white postcard-sized photo, its image possibly captured with my dad's Kodak 122 bellows camera, and its content attested to by that objective authority, my mother. The original photograph, alas, has disappeared and with it its clues of authenticity.

In the far background are low spruce trees above the riverbank. In the middle ground, sitting on the Chena River, is a sleek, striped, under-wing monoplane with huge floats. One of its cabin doors is open.

In the foreground, on the right, is Wiley Post, a short and husky, smiling man with a white patch over his left eye, luxuriant hair, and a short leather jacket, dark shirt, and dark knotted tie. On the left, a bit taller, is his grinning companion, Will Rogers, who is wearing a soft crusher hat, sports jacket, white shirt buttoned at the throat, and a dark vest.

In Rogers' arms, is a baby in overalls—me, according to my folks. The date was August 14, 1935, and I would have been one year, one month and ten days old, a moon-faced kid looking apprehensive and ready to pee his pants.

At this moment, Rogers and Post had about twenty-four hours to live.

I learned later that I wasn't the only Fairbanks kid that Rogers, with wit and grace, hefted from the crowd assembled to meet him and shake his hand that day. The world press had covered their around-the-world flight extensively, and their stop in Fairbanks was a big deal.

Rogers was the country's most beloved cowboy entertainer and newspaper wit. Post had earned international fame by flying around the world twice before, the first to do so. Although having been greeted by cheering crowds wherever he went, given medals by presidents, and having paraded down Broadway in a blizzard of confetti, Post struggled with his business ventures. This new world-circling flight to break his own speed record, Post hoped, would polish his reputation and attract financial support.

Rogers, an airplane buff, was Post's long-time pal. He even helped Post modify the new plane, the *Aurora Borealis*, and had commented on the size of the pontoons that Post had installed. The second-hand floats were so heavy that they narrowed the plane's margin of flying safety.

Many turned out to see the famous pair, including my mom and dad, with me. A large crowd of people and mosquitoes gathered on the riverbank that August evening, but Fairbanksans endured mosquitoes as a routine part of the universe. What could you do about them anyway except bitch?

Post was greeted by Joe Crosson, a Fairbanks bush pilot, famous himself for rescue, medical, mercy, and glacier flights.

The three daredevils posed on the float of the *Aurora Borealis* with another famous Fairbanksan, Leonhard Seppala, known to the world for his winter run with other dog mushers to deliver diphtheria vaccine to Nome in 1925.

Seppala and my dad were good friends, and Seppala had dined at our cabin many times. For years, we used his cabin at Cripple Creek on the Chatanika River north of Fairbanks, for grayling fishing in the summer and caribou hunting in the fall. (The cabin now is a state monument.)

Perhaps at my father's urging, Seppala persuaded Rogers to pose with me in his arms for my father's camera, if truly that was me in his arms. Who knows? I like to think that Rogers' magic touch imparted a tiny bit of his wit into my brain. Even so, as a newspaperman trained to doubt, I still wish I had the photograph to examine for its authenticity, if only so that I could flourish it as I bragged that Will Rogers himself had recognized my innate goodness and so had embraced me.

Because it was feared that with full gas tanks aboard, the *Aurora Borealis* might be too heavy for a safe takeoff from the narrow, twisting Chena River, the two men flew the next day to Harding Lake, fifty miles to the south, to take on gas there. Before a small audience of kids, they filled their tanks from gas trucked in barrels. Post used the big lake for a long runoff to lift the roaring, red and white craft into the air.

Post flew north toward their next stop, Barrow, on Alaska's north coast. On the way, Rogers probably hauled forth his portable typewriter to clack out his daily column to be telegraphed back to his newspaper syndicate for distribution. Rogers' column was the most popular in North America.

Just short of Barrow, the two men descended from heavy, low-lying clouds to land at Walakpa Bay, where they questioned Eskimo hunters about their whereabouts. The ceiling was getting lower, according to the hunters, but upon hearing that Barrow was only twelve miles away, Post and Rogers took off again. Just after the floats of the *Aurora Borealis* lifted off the lake and Post pulled the plane's nose up for altitude, the engine coughed and quit. The plane stalled, heeled, dropped, and slammed into the tundra. Many hours later, from one of the most isolated places on the globe, a news bulletin from the far north of Alaska shocked and saddened the world.

Wiley Post and Will Rogers were dead.

Seven

BREAKUP

My father gripped my hand as we stood where Wendell Avenue came to a dead-end at the river. Many others stood there, their voices barely heard over great grumbling and cracking. Huge chunks of the winter's ice were breaking up in a surge of snow melt. Dad lifted me onto his shoulder. Before us, dirty white slabs of ice reared and smashed amid excited laughter. We laugh at nature when it's not crushing us.

It was late April, bright and sunny and warm. Across the river at Graehl Landing, people lined the riverbank to watch this spectacle. It must have been a Sunday. Otherwise, my father wouldn't have been home so late in the morning.

Later, some strangers came to visit. My mother put out coffee and tea and cupcakes. They talked about a flood. Every time our door opened, we heard the roar of the ice. Each time it sounded closer.

After dinner, my dad and other men started digging a ditch around our house. The people next door, the Irwins, were digging, too. The ditches, I learned years later, had two purposes—to carry water away from the house toward low spots in the backyard and to supply dirt for dikes. Our Plymouth was gone. Dad had parked it a mile away on higher ground.

Inside, my mother, with help from other women, put our furniture up on concrete blocks. Our trunks were out. Clothes sat piled on the bed and the couch.

I was put to bed early. Out on the river, the ice was still grinding and smashing, and my mother began to cry. Dad, in hip boots and filthy with dirt, hugged her. Trunks went out the door.

I was snatched up. Mom, white-faced, quickly dressed me in coveralls, jacket, wool hat, and boots. Men shouted outside, and something thumped the cabin. The floor shook. Baby brother Buzz cried. The bow of a big outboard motorboat poked into the doorway. Dad handed me into the boat to one of my godfathers, Eddie Drouin. Eddie and my godmother, Mary Drouin, lived in a sunken log cabin full of wonderful smells two houses away, toward the river. Mom was sobbing. She had Buzz in her arms, wrapped in a blanket. In the boat sat a family with their luggage and trunks. Mom handed Buzz to a woman, then clambered in and took Buzz back. Eddie handed me to a man, who set me down next to Mom. She pulled me close. I looked around wide-eyed. We were in the river. Wendell Avenue flowed with water. A man in the boat pushed ice floes away with a long pole. I could feel Mom shaking.

Dad, in hip boots, had hopped into the boat after shoving off with one foot against the door frame. The front door yawned open. At the stern, Eddie Drouin pulled a lever, the motor roared, and the boat moved backwards, and then he eased the boat forward across the Irwins' front yard, around a fence, and then toward the ice. My dad and the other man shoved the ice aside with poles so the boat could pass through.

People were making funny sounds. The women looked pale.

We turned into Eddie Drouin's wood yard toward his three-story garage. Ice was scraping against it. On one side rose a wooden ladder nailed to the wall. Above, men peered down through an opening. Slowly the boat eased up to the garage. Someone tied the boat to the ladder with a rope.

Out of the door overhead stuck a big timber. I looked up, amazed. A big wheel was attached to one end, and a rope hung from the wheel, tied to what looked like a giant coal bucket that dangled to and fro.

"I can't get in that, Harry," my mother said.

"Yes you can, Eva. You won't be first. You won't be last. Kids first."

My mother's fright was contagious. The big bucket descended slowly, slowly, swaying. I heard a motor running inside. A chimney near the door puffed blue smoke.

"Stand in the middle and hold onto the sides," my father said as he lifted me into the bucket.

Someone let out a wail.

"I want to pee," I said.

"Up there," Dad said. His voice silenced any argument.

I grabbed the side of the bucket. The metal was cold.

"Haul away!"

My feet felt the bucket lift. I squeezed the sides. Dad's face grew smaller. All the faces in the boat looked up at me, frozen white, just staring.

"Here, boy." Big hands grabbed me under the shoulders and swung me into the doorway.

My feet hit a wooden floor. A noisy engine throbbed by the door. Another man took my hand and led me past stacked bales and boxes to another door. We entered a big shadowed room filled with men, women, children, and clothes drying on lines. A little light filtered through dirty windows along the far wall.

From a cord dangled a single light bulb over a big stove. Firewood was stacked on one side. I smelled food. A woman was cooking something on the stove, and I was hungry. People looked at me curiously, especially other kids. My mother walked in with my baby brother in her arms. She was shaking but smiling. People greeted her. Someone waved. She took me by the hand and they made space for us. The floor was covered with blankets. There were no chairs. Other people arrived. Mary Drouin, a short, fat, white-haired woman, smiled as she assigned people spaces that would be their temporary homes while we waited out the high water.

I asked Mom where Dad was. With Mr. Drouin, she said, they have to rescue other people.

The boat returned with more women and children and an old man. The boat departed again, and returned, and departed again. People kept coming. I was under Mom's orders to stay close. She took me to a gathering of women in a dark corner. The women talked about food. The garage shuddered whenever an ice slab slammed against the building, silencing all conversation for a few seconds.

People packed the room. At the far end, near a window, stood a big screen. Soon I smelled shit. The smell became powerful when my mother led me behind the screen to pee. A huge white enameled chamber pot was filled almost to the brim with pee and shit. I didn't want to get near it, but I had to pee. I knew Mom would switch me if I wet my pants, especially here, before other people. I peed but not happily. "Wait outside the screen," she said, "while I go too."

The stink stayed in my nostrils. Even when big pots of rice and beans started cooking on the stove, I could smell an undercurrent of shit.

Dad slogged in, drenched. "It's raining," he said. "Not good."

We ate out of bowls. I didn't like the food. No meat. But I ate after Mom flashed me a look that warned I best not complain.

I woke up, covered with blankets. Someone was sick, retching. “Mrs. Agbaba—flu,” Mom told Dad, who held me on his lap.

“Damn,” my father said. Ice banged into the building.

In the morning, Mom waved off the bowl of beans my father brought her. I ate mine. She staggered to her feet and rushed behind the screen, where I heard her retching. My dad went to stay with her while a lady sat with Buzz and me. Finally, Dad guided Mom back, his arm around her back and under an armpit, to hold her up. She was white and sweat covered her face. Dad laid her down, and then fetched her water. She pushed herself onto an elbow, drank with a shaking hand, slumped back down onto her blanket.

During the day, Dad tended to Mom and Buzz and kept me on a short leash. A line of desperate people waited to get behind the screen. Some of the men took turns emptying the chamber pot into the floodwater below. We children played, but sick people complained about the noise and commotion. We were allowed to look out at the town. Brown muddy water and hunks of ice and streams of slush surrounded the houses. Boats came and went in the rain. Men hauled up food in sacks and cases and wood for the stove. Medicines arrived in a big white box with a red cross on the side. Mrs. Drouin and Mrs. Korbo gave medicine and tea to my mother. Each kid received a piece of hard candy. I offered mine to Mom, who was on her back, sweating, looking up at the ceiling. She smiled and shook her head, patting my hand.

A man passed out, and great wailing erupted where he sprawled. I started to look, but a neighbor woman shushed me back to my mother, who slept. In the morning, the man was gone. My mother got better, but more people got sick. Each time I needed to pee or poop, I had to get in line, a new experience. Each time a lady I never saw again went with me, helping me to stand and keep my balance when I sat, so my butt wouldn't slip down into the filthy pot. Like everybody else, I became querulous. My dad, who in my childhood never spanked me, who never laid a hand upon me in anger, rebuked me for creating a fuss. A look from him, a word from him, hurt worse than a blow.

On the third day, we didn't hear the ice anymore. I looked out on a muddy world. The water had started to drop. My dad left with some men. After a while, we heard another big engine. It was Eddie Drouin driving a rubber-wheeled tractor that pulled a wooden-wheeled wagon through the flood waters. He taxied people to their homes, one family at a time. Finally our turn came. I went down in the bucket to where Dad lifted me into the wagon. Mom followed, with Buzz in her arms.

We slopped in mud to our cabin. My dad went in to have a look. I smelled not just mud, but rot. Dad emerged shaking his head and climbed back into the wagon. My mother cried, inconsolable. Eddie Drouin drove us along Wendell into town, where we got off at the Hunters' house. Bill and Maggie Hunter took us in. Their daughter Mary helped look after Buzz and me.

I don't know how long we stayed at the Hunters'. I have no memories of the stay, except that in the kitchen the Hunters had a big white box with a funny round thing on top that vibrated every now and then. I had never seen a refrigerator. We bought our ice from Smith's ice wagon, big chunks of river ice cut in winter that a man would lug in our front door with black tongs. But this magic box at the Hunters' made ice!

Finally we went home. Slippery mud covered the floors. The house stank. Mom attacked the mud with a broom. My dad waved her off and went to work with a coal shovel. My job was to open the street door as he emerged with a shovel full of mud, dumping it in the street. By then it was sunny out and warm. Robins hopped about in the mud covering the yard. We smelled cottonwood buds. Mom praised my work. For days she swept and mopped. And she went to other houses, too, to help other women. They came to our place to help Mom wash the walls and throw out the wet rug that they cut into pieces so that they could carry it out.

I played outdoors as the sun dried the earth. I thrilled at the approach of the town garbage wagon drawn by four big horses. The horses shit big lumps and pissed streams while they stood, their tails swishing away flies, as the driver and his helper loaded the hunks of wet rug, mucky blankets, mildewed clothes, and other debris stacked by the curbs.

God was in his heavens and all was right with the world.

Eight

A DROWNING

Mom was talking to someone at the front door. It was an overcast and muggy morning, common summer weather. I sat at the kitchen table on a chair stacked with pillows so that I could reach my favorite lunch, a lettuce and tomato sandwich. Brother Buzz sat in his high chair. We both wore shorts and a top, with no shoes.

Mom let out a yelp that scared me. I heard others crying and I got up to see what was the matter. Buzz started to bawl. Mom rushed into the kitchen wiping her hands on her white apron. She wore a flowered housedress and sandals. She always wore a housedress unless she was working in the garden, or picking berries, or picnicking, or camping. Then, she often wore cavalry pants with the ballooned sides, a shirt, and high brown leather boots.

She undid her apron, unhitched my brother from his highchair harness, put him under her arm, and grabbed my hand. "We have to go to the river," she said. "Donny's drowned."

I didn't know what drowned meant, but I understood it was bad.

Donny Irwin, who was five, lived next door. He was bigger than me. He lived in a house made out of lumber, with his dad and mom and sister Inez, who was my age.

Outdoors, we joined men and women hurrying down the dusty street amid much excitement to the muddy landing at the end of Wendell. Men with coiled ropes were launching a motor boat. Out on the river, several boats headed toward the mouth of Noyes Slough on the other side.

A long, loud howl of pain sounded behind us. My mother, with my brother and me in tow, turned around and hustled back. We went up the front steps into the Irwin home, passing through a windowed mud porch into the living room. The howl came from Donny's mom. Two ladies held onto her on a couch, rocking back and forth. Her face was all squeezed together, eyes shut, swollen, tears pouring from them, her mouth wide open and this terrible howl coming out of it. Buzz joined in. For once Mom didn't hush him. She put him down on the rug. "Hold on to him," she said.

Mom knelt in front of Mrs. Irwin and took her hands, kissing them. She said something. Mrs. Irwin rocked back and forth, up and down, and shook her head from side to side. She didn't speak, just howled. I heard a little voice crying somewhere else in the house. It might have been Inez.

Mom took us home. Neighbor women came and went, and then some men came back. They asked if Mr. Irwin had shown up. They had the body. They needed to know what he wanted done with it.

"Maybe the police know," my mother said.

"What police?" someone asked. I remembered the police from an earlier summer day. They had come for a run-over dog, fatally injured but not dead, writhing in the dusty street. One of the policemen pulled out his pistol, bent down, put it behind the dog's ears, and pulled the trigger. The bang startled me, but I was too amazed to care. The dog flopped, shuddered, and lay still. I went to inspect it, but Mom grabbed me and took me inside.

"It's dead," Mom had said. I wondered if the police would shoot Mrs. Irwin.

Suddenly, there was another commotion outside. I deserted my little brother on the floor and followed my mom.

"Oh! Oh! Oh!" Men surrounded Mr. Irwin, holding on to him. "Oh! Oh! Oh!" he kept repeating. "Oh! Oh! Oh! Goddamn it! Oh! Oh! Oh! Goddamn it!"

Mom shooed me back inside and soon Mrs. Korbo took charge of Buzz and me. Mom stayed at the Irwins. Through the window, I saw a police car arrive with a white ambulance bearing a red cross on the side. Everybody was headed to the Irwins. Then the police car and ambulance drove down to the river.

My dad came home early from the N.C. "I heard about the poor boy," he said. "The news is all over. Should I go next door?"

"Not yet," my mother said. "They took the body to the funeral parlor for the doctor to look at. Those poor people are in ruins."

I still didn't quite understand. I asked, "Is Donny dead?" I kept thinking of the dog run over in the street.

My dad said he was, poor boy. He'd gone across the river in a boat with some older boys to swim in the slough, but he didn't tell anyone that he couldn't swim. Donny hadn't told his mother where he was going. She wouldn't have let him go had she known.

On the slough, Donny had climbed into a tire tied to a rope hanging from a big cottonwood limb that jutted over the water. The tire swung back and forth and boys would jump from it into the murky water. Donny decided to try it.

"He didn't come up," Dad said. "His lungs filled with water. He couldn't breathe. His heart stopped. He died down there in the dirty water."

When Donny disappeared in the water, some of the boys dived in to find him, but they couldn't find him. Some of them swam across the slough to Graehl to get help. But nobody had a phone. It took a long time for somebody to drive to a phone and summon help. Meanwhile, Dad said, the boys came back over here in the boat but didn't tell Mrs. Irwin what happened. Instead, they ran to their homes and told their mothers. One of their mothers told some men in a bunkhouse down the street. They boated across the river and found Donny's body and brought it back before the police arrived, Dad said.

Mom said she and other women were fixing dinner for the Irwins. She took food to cook but soon came back. The Irwins didn't want food, she said. Their minister was with them.

People came and went at our house to talk about Donny. My mother was mad at the boys who took Donny across the river, but Dad said they didn't know any better. "Now they do," he said. "What happened will punish them enough."

Mom made coffee and put out cookies for visitors. Some had a drink with my dad in the kitchen. It was a long time before we had a chance to eat ourselves.

A couple of days later, Mom dressed me up and took Buzz to stay with Mrs. Korbo. After Dad came home, we went with the Coles—neighbors on the town side of our cabin—to a place half dark and smelling of the thick white flowers bunched along the wall. We sent flowers, Mom said, in memory of Donny. With other people, we sat in folding chairs before big black curtains. Two men in black suits came out. Each took hold of a curtain. They walked the curtains back to opposite walls.

On a stand draped with black cloth rested a big brown box with gold handles. Mr. and Mrs. Irwin, dressed all in black, came in and sat in front. I didn't see Inez. Behind us, music started. When I tried to turn around to see who and what was playing, Mom squeezed my arm. A minister came out. The adults all picked up books, opened them, and began to sing with the music. I couldn't see anything.

People cried. Mom sobbed and blew her nose on a white cloth hanky.

The minister said a prayer. I knew it was a prayer because we said the same prayer at the end of mass, all together. He talked about Donny, who was a good boy, an innocent boy. Donny was in heaven, happy, glad, and sitting with God. Donny was in the clouds, I knew, because I'd seen pictures of God sitting in the clouds as angels, like big white geese, flew around him on golden wings. Why was everybody so sad? Donny was an angel now.

The minister stopped. The adults sang again, a happy kind of tune. The Irwins rose up and went out, with men in black drawing them along. We rode with the Coles a few blocks to the Clay Street Cemetery.

I was hungry and tired, I didn't like standing in the hot sun while the minister talked again, and I was tired of holding mom's hand. There was another song. Mrs. Irwin was shaking and Mr. Irwin held onto her on one side, another man holding her on the other. Two men came forward and took up ropes. I was amazed. The box with Donny in it was going down into a hole in the ground. After another prayer, the minister picked up a handful of dirt and threw it into the hole. Mr. Irwin did the same. Mrs. Irwin kept shaking her head, no, no, no, no. Mr. Irwin talked into her ear, but she kept shaking her head. Finally he bent, picked up more dirt, and tossed it in the hole.

Mrs. Irwin wailed. Mom was sobbing.

After we got home, I thought about Donny. How cold it must be down there in a wood box in a black hole, covered with dirt. The next summer, the Irwins left Wendell Avenue forever. I still think about Donny. I remember a lean, smiling, black-haired boy, almost six, brown from the summer sun, never mean, always willing to play.

I've looked, but I can't find Donny's grave anymore.

Nine

GOING OUTSIDE

Buzz and I slept on a tan couch against a wall in the front room of the cabin. Every night, my mother pulled out the bottom of the couch, lifting it until it snapped into a bed. My brother slept on the inside. I slept with my head almost in the open doorway to our paents' bedroom.

Sometimes I awakened to hear Mom and Dad talk, or breathe deeply, or snore, or make love. Once, during lovemaking, Mom said, "It must be the vitamins that make us feel this way." Vitamins were new then.

Later, she said, "Not so fast. Not so fast. I'm not one of your girls of the street."

Their bed squeaked, and they groaned. Later, I'd see their ghostly white forms pass me and then I'd hear water running in the sink.

One night, a groan woke me. It was Dad. My mother cried out, "Harry! Harry! What's wrong?" Lights flicked on. Another groan. While Buzz slept on, I waited, frightened, as Mom thumped past me in her nightgown and went outdoors to the street. While she was gone, I heard, "Oh! Oh! Oh! Oh! Son of a bitch! Oh! Oh!" Dad moaned without stop.

Mom returned with Mrs. Korbo, whose pockets rattled with little bottles of medicine as she walked with a white towel wrapped around her head. I listened to them talking to Dad in the bedroom. Mom had called the doctor from the Coles' phone next door. Mrs. Korbo gave my dad something to drink. I heard him spit it up and groan again.

The doctor hustled by me with his black bag. Dad had quieted. Later, two men in white jackets came, carrying a gurney. I didn't know what was going on. Mom wept. The men in white jackets lugged my dad away. Right after that, Bill Hunter arrived. Mom, dressed by then, left with him. Mrs. Korbo sat down next to Buzz and me, singing words I didn't understand. Her palm on my forehead was smooth and warm.

Mom took Buzz and me to the hospital in a Pioneer Cab, its gray back seat soft and puffy and smelling of cigarettes. The hospital air smelled like church incense. We went up stairs and down a hallway that smelled funny, sweet but nasty.

My face was level with Dad's when he turned and smiled. He had black circles around his eyes and his lips were purple. When he reached his hand out to touch my cheek, I could see blue lines under his skin.

With the help of Mary Hunter, Mom packed our clothes into suitcases. Home from Saint Joseph's Hospital, Dad was thin and grim and rested most of the time in bed.

Bill Hunter drove us all to the stage station. That's what we called the bus depot. Mr. Hunter handed a man in a uniform some money and then supervised the loading of our luggage into the big yellow bus. In the waiting room, dusty with the silt that roiled up from the street every time a car went by, people crowded around a big radio in the corner where funny voices talked about war.

The bus rattled and rocked over the chuckholes as we drove down Cushman Street to the Richardson Highway. Gravel thrown up by the tires rattled around underneath the floorboard. After a while, I left my seat next to Dad and stood by the driver. He showed me the steering wheel, the gearshift, the handbrakes, and asked me to watch for moose.

It was hot in the bus. People kept the windows shut because if you opened them, dust from the highway boiled in. I soon tired of watching for moose and sat with Mom and Buzz while she read to us about gnomes and fairies and trolls and angels. Dad, wrapped in a blanket, slept. It wasn't noon yet.

Occasionally, we met cars or trucks coming at us. The road was so narrow that the driver geared the bus down to a creep and pulled over near the ditch to make room. One oncoming car passed so close everybody clapped after it got by.

Long after we passed Birch Lake, we stopped at a big muddy river and everybody got out. My dad smoked a King Edward cigar. Passengers lined up at a tin outhouse. Mom led me and Buzz into the bushes to pee. Mosquitoes swarmed, so we peed in a hurry.

A makeshift ferryboat with low, open sides pushed across the river's gray current, guided by a cable strung across the river. We climbed back in the bus. At the shore, the boat's front dropped so that cars and trucks could drive off. Then our driver rolled our bus onto the boat with a loud "clump, clump." The ramp came up. The boat's engine coughed blue smoke, roared to life, and the boat moved across in the current along the big cable. Everybody was quiet. It began to rain.

On the far shore we stopped at a two-story log roadhouse. Inside it was cool and dark. Places were set at a long table made of planks. After lunch, we resumed our long bus journey.

"Look, Johnny."

Dad shook me awake. Big icy mountains shimmered in the distance. Just ahead, the ground moved in waves of brown near a huge, round, treeless hill.

"Caribou," Dad said. My mother stood Buzz up on their seat to see them.

At first, I saw only a moving brown mass. Then I saw the individual animals. All the big ones had antlers.

"Wild reindeer," my dad said.

Beyond the dome-shaped hill, where the road ran over a big creek on a log bridge, caribou piled into the current to cross. The driver stopped and opened the door. We stepped out to watch. The passing bulls and cows and calves grunted and sighed, their antlers making clicking sounds when they touched. Each animal had big, bulging brown eyes. We laughed at the shit some dropped as they walked. The caribou didn't run but they kept moving. On the other side of the bridge, the passing herd blocked the highway.

We couldn't move. The driver said we'd be late for dinner at the next roadhouse.

We stopped at the Black Rapids Lodge, a low-lying log roadhouse with big rocks behind it and small birch trees all around. Across the highway, water the color of chocolate milk roared by in a fast-moving river, foaming over big rocks. I took Dad's hand as we stood on the riverbank. On the other side, under smudged clouds swirling just above our heads, loomed the bottoms of snowy mountains. The wind hurt, and it had started to snow. Dad limped as we returned to the lodge. Before we went inside, he fished a white pill from his vest and chewed it.

We joined mother and Buzz and the other passengers at a long table beside a tall fireplace made of black rock where a fire of spruce logs crackled and snapped. The room smelled of spruce pitch, hot bread, beer, and tobacco. The adults smoked and drank beer and whiskey. Buzz and I drank tart orange juice made from canned crystals and soda.

A waitress brought bowls of steaming beets and string beans, hot bread with butter, and caribou stew—chunks of potatoes, carrots, onions, and stringy meat in bubbling brown gravy. The fat lady who brought the food said the caribou had been killed and butchered just up the road that morning by the bartender and his brother. My mother forced Buzz and me to eat beets and beans.

We stayed overnight at Black Rapids in a small, chilly room, with two beds. I dropped off hearing the roar of the river and feeling its power vibrate the metal bed frame. Wind beat against the window.

Buzz and I huddled behind Mom, trying to hide from the gale. Others shivered behind the bus. The mountains, black at the bottom, snowy and icy above, their tops stuck in the clouds, loomed over us. Ahead of the bus, brown water rushed over the road. The driver, in hip boots, waded across, leaning on a big stick. A rope was tied to his waist. Barefooted men with their pants legs rolled up, including my father, kept the rope taut. Nobody talked.

Deeper and deeper the driver waded. The water rolled above his knees. He inched all the way across, turned, shrugged, and moved the knot on the rope around his waist. After wading back, the driver clambered into the bus followed by the women and kids. The men stayed outside to push the bus across the flooded road. My mother was not happy and said so. Dad's sick, she told other women.

"Don't worry," the driver said. "Holding onto the bus when they push will keep them safe."

He shifted into low gear, revved the engine. Dad and the other men shoved and moved with the bus. Into the stream we drove, the bus rocking in the heavy current. We bumped across. The women clapped and cheered. The driver opened the door and the men stomped in, wet over their knees, water draining off their pants. Dad and the other men took off their pants and wrung out the legs. Don't look, the driver laughed. Mom draped Dad's heavy coat over his shoulders. He put his pants back on, shivering, and wrapped his long coat about him. I went to sit with him and he gave me a squeeze.

I smelled salt water and seaweed for the first time. The smells excited my dad, the sailor. After dinner at the hotel in Valdez, where the blue water sat in a V of high, snowy mountains, Dad and I strolled down the main street onto a dock that stuck way out into the water.

A big ocean-going ship, the *Baranof*, the first I'd ever seen, laid against the dock, its engines humming over the wind and cries of gulls. As we approached, the ship grew higher and higher, like a giant wall. Bulging nets of cargo dropped onto the dock. Open wagons full of bags and boxes stood by, ready to be taken aboard. Men, with much shouting and waving, went up and down a gangplank with canvas sides.

In the middle of the night, we went down to the dock again and up the gangplank. At the top, a man in a blue uniform and blue hat, both with lots of gold trim, checked off our names on a clipboard.

Our stateroom was tiny and hot, and vibrated from the engines underfoot. It had two portholes and two bunks. I liked climbing up and down the ladder to the top bunk, where Buzz and I slept.

Through the soles of my tennis shoes I could feel the ship vibrate. When its whistle blew, I jammed my fingers into my ears. I loved the bells and gongs. Before every meal, a man in a white uniform, a steward, walked the passageways holding a rack of metal bars on which he bonged out a tune with a felt-tipped stick. The tune signaled grub. He called out the times for breakfast, lunch, or dinner for each passenger class.

We ate last. Almost every day when I heard the steward's bells, I trotted after him on my five-year-old legs. My father one day gave him money. After that, our steward kept checking to see if we needed anything.

Mom and Dad went ashore in Petersburg while a ship's lady looked after Buzz and me. When they returned, a wonderful smell flooded our stateroom, oh, a smell of exceeding delight. On the floor sat a small gunnysack of red, still-steaming crabs, the first fresh crabs Dad had seen in ten years and the first I'd seen ever.

Mother opened the other packages and pulled out fresh bread, Velveeta cheese, mayonnaise, Cokes, beer, paper plates and napkins. We were going to have a picnic.

Dad dumped the crabs into the sink. He grabbed a crab and, with a pull and a twist, shook out its guts. He cleaned them all, piling the good parts on another bag. The guts he tossed out a porthole to a chorus of gulls. Buzz and I examined the big claws.

Dad cracked the crab legs with a shoe. Mom offered Buzz and me pieces of white, red-veined meat with buttered bread and Cokes. Wonderful. She and Dad set to, with beer. We skipped shipboard lunch that day.

The dock at Seattle, smelling of diesel oil, swirled with gulls. People milled and shouted and shoved. Dad didn't feel well. Mom gave a porter some money. He rolled our luggage on a hand trolley to a cabstand. We were taken to a hotel where a calico cat slept on the reception desk. A doctor visited our room and from a black bag removed a big jar of white pills. Dad took several and slept.

I sat by the window, watching the train's engine belch black smoke as it pulled the passenger cars through the forest and mountains. That night, Buzz and I climbed a ladder to sleep in the top berth. I stared at the black man in a white jacket who helped us get settled. He resembled the black men who worked in the swaying restaurant car.

"He's a darky, a porter," my mother said. I didn't know what a porter was but his black skin fascinated me. He gave Buzz and me suckers with a picture of a steam locomotive on the wrapper. My mother and father talked about how much money to give him. My mother hated to tip. "Nobody tips me," she said. As we got off the train, my father handed the porter a bill, and the black man's smile lit the gloom of the railroad station.

In San Francisco, we went to 326 Waller Street, one block south of Haight and Fillmore. Behind a high metal mesh fence was a white-graveled walk with tall flowers blooming on both sides. Where the walk ended, flights of stairs rose to the left and to the right of a tall yellow building. As the cab drove off, Mom fretted because nobody had come out to meet us. I held onto the hem of Dad's suit jacket, surrounded by suitcases. He lifted a latch, opened the metal gate, and pulled our luggage through. We rang a doorbell.

Dan and Mary Delaney, and Aunt Marguerite Delaney opened their door with exclamations of joy and kisses. They lived in a second-story flat. The door opened into a narrow, dark, high-ceilinged hallway with walls of dun metal stamped with fleur-de-lis, just like in our cabin. I learned about fleur-de-lis from Aunt Marguerite, who said they were a sign of royalty, and laughed.

Grandpa Delaney was short and stumpy with a smiling, wide, red-cheeked face. He wore black ankle-high shoes, black pants, a white shirt, a green tie, and black suspenders. Gray and white smudged his black hair, which lay flat on his head. Grandma Delaney stood even shorter. Her broad, smiling face was covered with powder, I noticed, as she squatted to kiss me.

She had a funny hat, like a big white sock, and between her blue eyes was a very sharp nose, like my mother's. I thought my grandpa and grandma looked like the dwarves in "Snow White." And Aunt Marguerite reminded me of Snow White.

Aunt Marguerite couldn't bend down to greet me and Buzz. She stood on crutches, her hands twisted at the wrists, where she gripped the handles. Her face in repose looked pinched, but when she smiled, the sun came out. And her voice was oh so sweet. Leaning on one crutch, she held out a hand to caress my forehead. All her fingers crooked in toward her palm. Her knuckles glowed red, but her lips were white.

We settled in. My grandpa produced a bottle and glasses. Dad was very tired and sat down as soon as he could. Grandmother poured coffee from a huge metal pot that bubbled on the gas stove in the tiny kitchen. The adults had coffee and whiskey, except for Marguerite. "I have a hard time holding a cup," she said. Buzz and I drank Coke.

The flat seemed stuffed. Except for the light coming in through the south windows of the living room, the place dripped gloom. It consisted of a small hallway, living room, dining room, tiny kitchen with a door opening onto a fire escape, and a small bathroom with a white tub that stood on curled legs. In the bathroom, Grandpa had built a throne with a special wooden seat for Marguerite because it hurt her to sit down too low. She had a special chair in the kitchen, too, and one in the dining room and one in the living room, each piled with pillows and fitted with wooden handles made by Grandpa so she could rest without pain. There were two bedrooms, one with a special bed for Marguerite, both in shadows and half-light from small, high windows.

They liked the place, Grandma told me more than once, because everybody for blocks around was Irish, even the priest who came every morning to give Marguerite confession—bless her—and put a wafer on her tongue. Day after day, I watched for all the sins Marguerite was committing, sins so bad that a priest had to come see her every day so she would not die and go to Hell. Afterwards, the priest would have a drink with Grandpa, and listen to Grandma.

Grandma liked to talk. Morning after morning, I'd hear her as I awoke from the couch-bed where Buzz and I slept in the living room. Mom and Dad slept on a similar couch. Sometimes I would get up and join Grandma in the kitchen while the coffee perked. On a table sat a tall radio much like the wooden Zenith we had at home.

The first day after we moved into 326 Waller Street, we all walked over to Fillmore to ride a streetcar. This was a thrill. The car rumbled, creaked, groaned, squeaked, and moaned down the hill. When we got off, my dad moved us all to where we could catch the L Car for an even greater pleasure—riding through the tunnel under Twin Peaks. That scared Buzz and he squawked. Mom soothed him. The black maw of the tunnel, the rumble of the streetcar, the sudden darkness ruined only by pinpoints of electric lights, the clang and clacking, the acrid smell of sparks spitting from electric contacts, was an adventure I relished. I laughed and sang and soon discovered that other passengers would give me money if I just asked for it. What I thought was money turned out to be official-looking multi-colored transfer slips.

Shortly after the L Car emerged from the tunnel on the west side of Twin Peaks, and after a turn here and there, it continued its stop-and-go journey down Taraval Street toward the ocean. At Twenty-Fourth and Taraval, uphill and across the street from a park, we came to a building with two flats over a garage. My father rang the buzzer. Soon the door opened, and there stood a tall, fine-looking, gray-haired woman who turned out to be Aunt Lou, my father's sister. Behind her, looking down, in white loose vestments, yoo-hooing, waving and smiling was another handsome woman, much older, who braced against a balustrade, holding a cane. This was Aunt Dora, my dad's half-sister. Around her peered the homely face of my cousin Dorothy—"Dora's girl," as my mom called her. Dorothy was then in her thirties.

We walked into what appeared to me to be a place of luxury with thick rugs, chandeliers, vases of cut flowers scenting the rooms, and a polished player piano on which ghostly fingers played one hundred tunes. Everything was immaculate.

At first, my aunts doted on my brother Buzz and me but soon we learned that Aunt Lou pulled the ears of little boys who messed throw rugs and made too much racket. Still, ample refreshments including candies appeared, jacking up the sugar in our youthful circulation systems. Soon there took place what puzzled me that summer—a clash of views between Lou and my mother, with Dora interjecting, trying to change subjects and my dad avoiding the chief subject over which two strong-willed women wrestled, that being religion.

It took no genius to learn that Aunt Lou thought Catholicism was a quaint superstition and that my mother thought Aunt Lou was a patronizing bitch.

(Years later, I came to understand that Lou had led the opposition in the de Yonge family to her brother marrying a lace-curtain Irish woman who revered the Pope, and that, worse, my dad, then in his fifties, after some consequential exchange, had not so politely told Lou to fuck off. I also came to understand that my mother never forgot and rarely forgave a slight. Deep within her flashed genes selected by thousands of years of Celtic experience that said if someone punches your nose, you stick a sword in their eye.)

My Cousin Dorothy unsettled me far more than Aunt Marguerite. Dorothy talked funny. She moved on shoes full of rocks. Her face sprouted whiskers. Her clothes looked too big. She laughed with big yelps. And I learned that if you pushed her, she'd snap back and sometimes charge with flashing eyes. I never feared her, but I kept my eye on her, as one would with a big dog that didn't grin.

After lunch at Dora and Lou's, we took a cab to another home in the Taraval District, that of my Aunt Etta. Like Aunt Dora, Etta had married a Liebe brother. The brothers had died young, first Dora's husband, then Etta's. After her husband died, Etta married a Hahn, who also had died by the time I arrived. In contrast to her sisters, Aunt Etta was short and stubby. In her house, she was perpetually busy, always kind and cheerful. She had a difficult time staying in one place, even as she served refreshments that included cookies that to this day rank high within my pantheon of cookies, cookies being one of the few things on earth that make living seem worthwhile.

Etta had one son, George, one of the best-dressed and most handsome men on the San Francisco social scene. He was a top salesman at Roos Brothers, in that day a San Francisco equal to Brooks Brothers and Abercrombie & Fitch. George played tennis with his rare, handsome and bird-like wife, Alma, who was an officer at Wells Fargo Bank. In 1939, a time when women were relegated to menial tasks, she had risen to be a vice-president dealing with major accounts. George and Alma were childless, not by design I think now, but by faults of nature. When we visited, they both doted on me and my brother. My dad and George devoted much of their talk to fly-fishing. George was a good cousin, an adult favoring a small boy.

However, with George and Alma, as with the rest of my father's family that summer, my mother seemed uneasy. George and Alma personified the gay couple from the Jazz Age, which they were, living a life of leisure and culture foreign to Mom. George and Alma drank and dined with some of San Francisco's leading citizens. To Mom, they seemed like actors in a movie. They ceremoniously mixed martinis, pouring them from a frosted silver chalice into chilled long-stemmed glasses. They wore fine clothes, even at home with family. George looked freshly shaved, Alma freshly coiffed. Alma smoked cigarettes from a long, black cigarette holder.

Mom always reported to her family every rich detail of a visit with the charmed and charming pair.

Ten

DAD'S SURGERY

I didn't fully understand until years later that my father had been very ill from kidney stones, and that we had traveled to San Francisco not to visit kin, but for him to endure an operation at a major hospital that was better staffed and offered more advanced treatment than Saint Joseph's.

Mortal danger attended the operation. Doctors then did not have penicillin at hand, or any other natural or synthetic antibiotics of the kind we use routinely today. The Germans were perfecting sulfa drugs, chemicals to put on wounds to prevent or limit some infections. Although the research was published in 1935, thanks to Hitler, the Nazi regime through patents and other rigmarole tried to restrict the use and clinical knowledge of sulfanilamide, knowing that having exclusive use of this antibiotic would give advantage to the Germans in treating battlefield wounds and returning wounded soldiers to battle. Hitler always thought ahead.

Consequently, the danger of infection attended surgery. Many patients died of "blood poisoning." In those days, only dire need caused one to undergo the scalpel.

To forestall infections, surgeons practiced minimalism: They trained to make the smallest incision necessary to reach an inflicted area and they trained to cut, fix and sew as fast as possible. (I knew a major surgeon who trained in Budapest for speed and agility just as Hitler was marching into Austria next door. My friend said he could incise, remove an appendix, sew up the patient, and pat him on the forehead—all in five minutes. Even so, many died of peritonitis.)

Another danger was diethyl ether—the major anesthetic of the day, a highly volatile liquid whose vapors will send a human into a profound stupor, during which the brain would register no conscious pain. Ether, however, is flammable and explosive. Hospitals designed operating rooms as if they were storing gunpowder. Surgical teams wore gowns and slippers to prevent sparks. Furthermore, ether stressed the heart and could kill a weak patient and cause other patients to awake retching, with profound hangovers, as I was to learn myself decades later.

When Dad went away with Mom to the hospital, after many visits to doctors on Market Street, worry infected the Delaney domain. I didn't understand it but I could feel it. Mom looked drained. She was at the hospital when the surgeons cut and sliced.

Mom showed up the next day. She had stayed overnight while Dad was in a recovery room. He was fine, she said, but not happy. Hospitals required long stays after a major operation then. Weeks passed before Dad, thin and gray looking, could get up and chat with us when we came to his room. Our mother exercised wisdom in not taking Buzz and me to see Dad until he regained his sense of humor and laughter.

Dad could not travel yet. After leaving the hospital, he had to see the doctor again, first two or three times a week, then twice a week. Finally he talked about going home. But first he wanted us to see the San Francisco World Fair, formally the San Francisco International Exposition of 1939.

The thing I most remember about the fair was seeing the China Clipper, a giant flying boat built for Pan American World Airways by the Glenn L. Martin Company that lumbered off each day with a load of well-dressed passengers to fly across the Pacific Ocean to Manila in the Philippines, with stops in Hawaii, Midway Island, Wake Island, and Guam—names that war soon would imprint on the American consciousness.

To me, this great white boat with wings dwarfed the rest of the world. Onlookers stood behind a rope while the handsomely uniformed crew welcomed men and women in suits and dress shoes onboard. Trunks and suitcases were loaded through a big door in the plane's side. All the while someone on a microphone related minute by minute what was going on.

Mom held Buzz up so that he could see. Dad elevated me, a sacrifice in comfort I'm sure, considering his physical condition and my husky size.

At last, the gangplank lifted. Doors slammed. On the dock, the ground crew dressed in white coveralls waved a signal. Way up there in a tiny square window, the pilot signaled back. One engine sputtered, coughed, smoked, and roared to life; then another engine, and another, and yet another.

I laughed with pleasure as the plane eased forward toward San Francisco Bay, the powerful wind from its propellers blowing back on us. Whitecaps danced out on the bay.

Dad said he bet that some passengers would get seasick before the bobbing plane lifted. At last, way off in the distance, the white plane accelerated with a great roar of its engines, a long wake trailing behind it as it slammed into the waves. What a sight! Finally, the flying boat lifted into the air, slowly, then faster, until it became a white dot on the horizon.

Dad bought two small turtles for Buzz and me after much pleading. One displayed Dopey from "Snow White" painted on its back. My turtle showed Smiley grinning up. One day, as my mother fussed about with her mother, packing our trunks, Dad said he was taking me back out to Steinhart's Aquarium at Golden Gate Park. We went by streetcar. Dad carried a paper bag that I thought was lunch. At the aquarium, we went to a big pool full of alligators, crocodiles, and other reptiles.

Dad maneuvered us up to the ropes that kept viewers back from the pool's edge. Suddenly, something splashed at our feet. I looked down. Dopey was sinking out of sight. Horrified and amazed, I saw another splash of water. Smiley looked up at me, and then paddled away. I sobbed.

"Smiley, Smiley!" I yelled.

"He's better off here than being flushed down the toilet," Dad said. "We can't take them with us."

His words did not comfort. I feared a crocodile would slide forward, jaw open, to crunch Smiley with a smile. I caterwauled. Dad took me outdoors into Golden Gate Park. A hotdog would not placate me. A cone of spun sugar reduced my keening. Finally, an ice cream ended my mourning.

Thirty-five years later, when I took my own son, John, to the aquarium, as I was showing him the very same reptile pool where his granddad's dastardly deed was done, I noticed a turtle sunning himself on a rock. I swear, though the paint was gone from his back, it was Smiley—bigger, fit, and looking contented. The de Yonges had made a permanent contribution to the aquarium.

Eleven

KILLER WHALES

In that fall of 1939, despite being up and around and being able to take us to the San Francisco fair, the zoo, and the aquarium, my father looked like he was wearing a suit two sizes too large. The operation to remove kidney stones had thinned him, and his height made him seem even thinner. He joked that we should call him "Skinny," a nickname common then when few people ate enough to be fat.

In my grandparents' flat on Waller Street, something important was going on. Hour after hour, Grandpa and Grandma and sometimes Aunt Marguerite and my mom and dad clustered around the radio. Hitler, with his partner in butchery, Joseph Stalin, had invaded Poland. France and England declared war against Nazi Germany, but not Stalin's Soviet Union.

My grandparents cared little about what happened to the Poles, though Poles were Catholics, too. But Dan and Mary

Delaney and Marguerite and my mother yearned for one thing: for the perfidious English, oppressors of the Irish for seven hundred years, to get their tails whipped bloody. It had only been twenty years earlier that the British and Irish had terrorized, tortured, and killed each other on Irish soil in a war that resulted in creation of the Irish Free State in Ireland's south, but no independence for Ireland's northern counties. If it took a crazy man like Hitler to chastise England, so be it; God willed it. Mom and her folks praised brave little Ireland for declaring its neutrality the minute the war started, despite the risk that the English might march south out of the northern counties to try again to conquer the Catholic south.

(Winston Churchill, after becoming England's prime minister, wanted to do just that: take over neutral Ireland. He backed off after President Franklin Roosevelt warned him against it. "Kill the English bastards" remained the Delaney prayer for Hitler until Germany declared war on the United States two years later. I carried the Delaney opinion of the English and the Germans with me into my first years of school. These opinions didn't matter much until our country went to war. Then my classmates bloodied my nose and changed my mind.)

Finally, the San Francisco doctors told my dad he could return north. We hurried to pack. I was late for kindergarten in Fairbanks. My father had not had a paycheck in months. In 1939, only a handful of princes enjoyed sick leave and none of them lived where we did. Get sick? Watch your income shrivel, and suffer. That was the American way of life that Republicans have fought to preserve ever since.

We traveled by train back to Seattle, where we boarded an Alaska Steamship Line steamer, the *Denali*. Dad pointed out the immense American flags painted on both sides of the ship. Huge flags flew from the three masts—one at the bow, one by the funnel, and another at the fantail. Before dusk, spotlights snapped on to illuminate the flags. Dad explained what I vaguely understood, and what my mom nattered about, that a German submarine might torpedo the ship and drown us all if the sub mistook the *Denali* for a Canadian or other ship from the British Empire. I knew that the British Empire was red, having seen it on my grandfather's world globe. He allowed Buzz and me to spin it and then would ask us to find San Francisco, Fairbanks, and Dublin, the three most important places in the world.

We threw confetti over the side at people waving below as the *Denali* churned away from the dock. Lifeboat drills came next. On command, my dad snatched me, my mother grabbed Buzz, and they strode with other hustling passengers to where the de Yonges would muster to board a lifeboat should a German torpedo blast the *Denali*. The drills occurred over and over as the ship plowed northward. At the dining tables, my folks talked with other passengers about the war. They laughed at the idea that the *Denali* was at risk. Being an American ship made it immune from German attacks, they thought. My parents held to the predominant view that Uncle Sam had no dog in the renewed fight among the ferocious Germans, the perfidious English, and the lazy French. Years later, I learned the Germans in World War II mounted no submarine warfare along the West Coast of North America.

It wasn't that they didn't want to. They couldn't.

After several days at sea, the *Denali* began to move in all directions at once. During breakfast, with blasts of salty wind rushing in each time a deck door opened, the crew entered the dining room to secure tables, chairs, and other furnishings. I was amused to see the milk in my cup rise up one side and then the other and to watch salt and pepper shakers slide back and forth. People rose from breakfast before finishing the last of their bacon and eggs, my mother among them. With her went Buzz, who had assumed a squid's pallor.

My dad, the old sailor, rejoiced in the storm as he escorted us to our stateroom while the ship went up and down and pivoted and rolled from side to side. Walking the narrow passages back to the stateroom we were flung from side to side. Mom put Buzz in a bunk, where he puked immediately. After she cleaned him, Mom collapsed onto the lower bunk. I retreated with Dad, clutching his hand to keep from falling.

Outside, he gripped my arm. With satisfaction on his haggard face that I still see to this day, we staggered forward, a tall old man and a little boy, wind whipped, to view great waves swelling into foam-topped mountains before they crashed over the bow and swept the lower decks with great washes of green, cold water. I shivered in the gale as waves pounded the boat. Flurries of rain machine-gunned us. At that, we retreated to the salon dining room, where Dad wrenched the door open and hustled us inside just before the ship heeled and the door slammed shut. We grabbed rails along the walls. All the other passengers had fled to their staterooms. Wan sailors battened down anything that could move, including the grand piano.

An officer lurched up to us and after some conversation, invited us to the wheelhouse. Years later, my dad explained that he and I were the only passengers then not prostrate with seasickness. Even so, he counted the invitation a special honor bestowed upon an old sailor and his son.

From my perspective at the level of my dad's hip, I looked up at the helmsman spinning the ship's wheel to confront every wave. The captain issued orders in a low voice. A sailor repeated them into tubes running into the floor. Against the square windows where wipers swept back and forth, black water assaulted us in relentless waves. The captain turned, smiled, and invited us to join him and other crew members in donning life preservers fetched by a sailor.

My life vest was too big. The captain discussed this with my dad. About then, I became dizzy and threw up on my dad's trousers. Laughing, he gathered me up. With a sailor summoned by the captain to escort Dad and me, we reeled to our stateroom. When the sailor opened the door, the smell of vomit rolled out and we heard retching. I joined my mother and brother in the pleasures of puking. For several eternities, too weak to move, I lay beside my brother and we both peed and crapped our pants. Dad washed and changed us, wiped our faces with lemon-scented water, and forced all of us including Mom to take water. She told me years later that had she a pistol, she would have cured her seasickness right then with a bullet. Our agonies lasted three days, she said, as the *Denali* fought the storm without making much headway. Dad took meals with the captain and other officers. Those hours he didn't spend caring for us he spent in the wheelhouse, sharing stories with professionals about the sailor's life he had foresworn.

Finally, the wind died, the waves shrank, and the ship steadied. Our nausea subsided. Even while we still lay abed wondering whether we had strength to stand, stewards came in and swabbed, tidied, and wiped, replacing linen and opening the portholes to freshen the cabin. Eventually, the wan de Yonges arose to rejoin humanity.

The sun came out. The wind whispered. Passengers in overcoats lolled in deck chairs again or strolled along the deck. On one of these walks savored by my dad, he yelled suddenly: "Look! Look!" He pointed toward the mountains. "Killer whales!"

He hoisted me to his shoulder. Mom lifted Buzz. Fellow passengers jammed to the rails.

The water exploded as a great gray whale rose from the ocean, a vivid giant, seeming to stand there on its tail, its jaws wide, pink tongue protruding. From that tongue hung a much smaller black and white fish—I thought it was a fish—shaking and waving, its tail out of the water. Blood sprayed from the whale's tongue.

It was a shocking sight. Another black and white "fish"—a killer whale, an Orca—jumped to grab the gray whale's tongue just as the giant beast smashed back into the sea. Hundreds of white birds wheeled and cried, diving into the reddening water. The Gray Whale breeched again, an orca fastened onto flesh on the great whale's side. As the whale powered upward, the force of its movement against the killer whale's teeth and weight stripped away skin and blubber. Three orcas held onto the big whale's tongue, and the blood flowed. All around, other orcas closed in for the kill.

The ship turned toward the battle and stopped. Each time the gray whale thrashed out of the bloody water, I saw a giant eye, a bloodshot orb that looms yet in my dreams about the fairness of life.

The whale leaped no more. It whipped and thrashed on the surface. A dozen orcas attacked. Blubber was stripped white. Blood pooled the ocean.

How long did this orgy of death, this natural devouring of the one greater by the many smaller, continue? I don't remember. Certainly longer than it takes to stun and cut the throat of a bawling veal or a bleating lamb.

The gray whale's agony continued as the *Denali* turned away and continued up Prince William Sound to the snow-sprinkled mountains surrounding old Valdez, where we disembarked for our long, bumpy bus ride home.

Twelve

KINDERGARTEN

From our cabin's kitchen, a little light and a clanging sound spilled into the far end of the living room. I peered out from the tunnel I'd made of blankets and a sleeping bag piled atop Buzz and me.

Shivering, I sniffed the sulphur of a match. My dad had lit a wood fire in the small stove we called the trash burner and dropped the lid back on with another clang. Then he started the other wood fire that he had laid the night before in the big kitchen range. He adjusted the chain that ran through a hole in the kitchen floor to the furnace in the cellar. The cellar door squeaked open. He descended into that dark hole with a flashlight to light the new furnace. It burned hunks of sawed and chopped birch stacked alongside the cabin.

I snuggled down to sleep again. It would take a long time for the cabin to warm. I shivered again when Mom rousted me from bed and put a robe over my long, itchy wool underwear.

For breakfast we had canned grapefruit or peaches, steaming oatmeal doused with brown sugar and thin milk my mom mixed from white powder, toast fried on a hot stove lid, and blueberry jam from the berries we picked that fall.

My dad, already dressed in wool whipcord pants and a light, plaid wool shirt, donned his down parka and mink hat with the big earflaps, each with a tasseled cord that you could tie under your chin. He pulled on wool gloves, slipping them and his parka sleeves into moosehide mittens that hung from a cord around his neck. The mittens reached from his fingertips almost to his shoulders. Finally, he stomped the black leather shoes he always wore into sheepskin-lined rubber overshoes and kissed us goodbye.

When he opened the front door, freezing fog rolled into the cabin, and he trudged off into the December darkness. At its peak, if the ice fog cleared, the sun might glow faintly low in the southern sky just before noon. Dark fell soon after lunch.

Mrs. Korbo came over from across the street to look after Buzz, who still slept, hurrying because she wore only her indoor clothes—a big black dress down to her shoes, with a high neck and long sleeves, and a smooth white cloth over her head, soft, not stiff like the nuns wore. What women wear in Finland, Mom said.

Mrs. Korbo helped dress me in wool pants, wool shirt, blue wool sweater that she had knit for me, wool socks to my knees, Indian moosehide moccasins stuffed with wool insoles; a green wool, pull-down hat Mom made; a heavy, red and black checkered wool coat with its big collar flipped up higher than my ears, such that I seemed to be staring out of a closet. One wool muffler went around my neck inside the coat. The other went around the collar on the outside, and Mom tied it so that she could pull it up over my mouth and nose. With the hat pulled over my eyebrows, I viewed the world through a narrow slit. My hands in red wool mittens dove into moosehide mittens that, like my Dad's, came almost to my shoulders. A leather thong tied the mittens together. It hung around my neck. I was ready to go to kindergarten.

My mom dressed like Dad, her sheepskin-lined overshoes zippered up, topped with a wide sheepskin ruff that circled her lower calves where her wool slacks were tucked in.

The front door opened and once again wisps of icy fog poured in. Before I'd taken ten steps, holding my mother's hand, my nose tingled with cold. We marched resolutely in the foggy darkness, a tan glow cast by a single bulb atop a telephone pole in each intersection, passing houses whose light strained through thick coatings of ice on the windows.

We trudged in fog thick, gray, and dirty with wood and coal soot from stoves and coal smoke from the N.C. power plant. The fog also stunk of gasoline and diesel fumes from car and truck engines. In the gloom, as a vehicle neared, all I could see was a diffused headlight gleam that grew larger and larger. Few cars ran when it was forty below. No trucker shut off a diesel engine in that kind of weather. Fairbanks had no school buses.

Mom walked me along, sticking to sidewalks that were clear of snow and ice; otherwise, we walked in the street. We made our way down Wendell and up Noble Street, turning right onto Second Avenue, where the new movie theater was. We passed the brighter lights from the storefronts, bars, the Nordale Hotel, the Co-Op Drug, and big Model Café. In the fog, figures appeared and disappeared. Nobody stopped to chat.

Mom told me, "Don't breathe through your mouth. Your lungs will freeze. You don't want your lungs to freeze, do you? Breathe through your nose."

She was down on frozen lungs, and I didn't want her down on me because I had acquired one. So, I said, "No, mama . . . no, mama . . ." whenever she warned me. I learned not to complain, though the cold hurt my face. My breath froze the scarf over my mouth, stiff and hard. The ice crystals rubbed my skin. When I sniffed, I felt my nose hairs freeze. That hurt. The cold clutched my eyes. The first time, I complained and cried, but that made Mom angry. "Nothing we can do about it. Nothing we can do about it. We'll be at the Post Office soon."

The Post Office was in the four-story Federal Building at Second Avenue and Cushman Street, the main intersection in town. We had to be careful crossing Cushman because it was covered with hard ice formed into slippery ruts and ridges from passing cars and trucks. We both hurt with cold.

Climbing the Federal Building's steps, we hurried through the first of the three great doors facing the street. As soon as we stepped in, we felt heat from steam radiators in the entryways. Then we passed through another door onto a flight of marble stairs rising to a most wondrous device, an elevator with wonderful ornaments on its door. We rarely went up those stairs. Mom would check our mail box on the way back home. Instead, we loitered by the steam radiators. Mom shed her mittens and untied my outside scarf, spreading it on top of one of the radiators. If there was room, other mothers and kids gathered there too. I learned that the heat would melt the ice. We didn't stay long enough to dry the scarf. It would be hot and wet when she tied it back on, but soon became cold and wet, and then cold and frozen.

Sometimes, two or three mothers rebundled their children at the same time, and then we all walked the last five blocks to Main School together. Mom and I were a mile from home.

On some days, winos stinking in the heat blocked us from the radiators. The women scolded them. But drunks with no houses and no place to go knew that being jawed at by decent citizens was a small price to pay for staying warm and alive when it was forty below.

Having warmed up in the Federal Building, we plunged again into the bitter cold, crunching south on Cushman Street, passing a clutch of small stores before we crossed Fourth Avenue, a block east of the Whore Line, as people called it. For some years, I wondered what kind of a line a whore was.

Next, we passed City Hall where red fire trucks stood ready behind the shiny great doors. Finally, we rounded the corner at Eighth Avenue to see the lights of Main School. It housed kindergarten in the basement along with the elementary-school classes. The two upper stories of the huge concrete structure housed middle grades, the nurse's and the superintendent's offices, and the high school. In the rear, the combined gymnasium-auditorium had tall, dividing doors that closed like an accordion against the walls to create one big space. The building had a confusing maze of hallways and stairways.

Mom had walked me to Main School for the first time in September. She escorted me down the inside stairs to the basement kindergarten room, where a tall, gray-haired lady with glasses held sway. This was my first teacher, Miss Ross. After a few weeks of classes, Mom loosened her hold of my hand once we got into the school, saying goodbye, and I'd scamper by myself downstairs to the marvels I had experienced in kindergarten.

By Thanksgiving, when Fairbanksans bundled themselves against the fierce cold, I learned to unknot that damned cold, ice-stiff scarf as soon as I was out of Mom's sight. Miss Ross, however, insisted on helping us with our layers of clothes, and then supervised us as we hung them up on reserved wooden pegs in a narrow cloakroom. Life pegged us early.

Like other kids who showed up in Indian moccasins, a sign of poverty almost as obvious as coming with feet freezing in rubber-bottomed shoepacs, I had to remove my moccasins and heavy socks, pull on light socks and leather shoes the school required Mom to leave there, despite her grumbles about the cost and fear someone would steal them. Kids from prosperous families arrived at school in leather shoes and sheepskin-lined overshoes. Administrators preached that wearing outdoor winter footgear and socks in the classrooms caused the feet to sweat, nourishing a horror and a disgrace—Athlete's Foot. Periodically, they'd line us up, barefoot, to inspect between our toes, in case one of us had footed this leprous ailment into the room. We joked about toe jam.

The kindergarten windows peered out at ground height. During daylight, we could see the feet of passersby.

A piano sat in the front of the room, near the teacher's desk. Movable wooden shelves stood full of necessities—tambourines, cymbals for dinging with small metal rods, midget drums, notched dowels for scraping, all for our rhythm band; wooden blocks with the ABCs on them and numbers zero to nine; boxes of Tinker Toys, several Erector Sets; colorful picture-books full of dogs and cats and moo cows and horsies and zebras and elephants and lions and tigers with their names printed under them in big letters; and small pillows for our daily naps on mats we'd take from a stack against the back wall. Also furnishing the classroom were tiny chairs, little tables, and what I thought then to be the greatest invention of humankind—the sandbox.

My education started in the sandbox. We didn't have sand on Wendell Avenue, we had flood silt and dust and I enjoyed them both, but real sand was something else. When I first saw it and felt it, shyly, I held back because on the first day of school other boys and some girls already sat in the big box making piles, shoving toys through the sand, and using spoons to shovel sand into walls.

When I hopped into the box, I plopped down beside a boy named Ray who looked like me, except he was taller, with a round head and blond, nearly white hair, brown eyes, and broader shoulders. I reached for a block in the sand and he snatched it out of my hand. I recoiled, shocked. I hefted another block. He reached for it. I hit his hand with the block. He snarled and punched my cheek. I yelped and hit him back in the cheek. He lunged, grappled me, and as the sand flew, the girls nearby screamed. Suddenly, a hand on my shirt hauled me up as I punched and kicked air. With her other hand, Miss Ross hoisted my flailing opponent. She dropped us on our feet and grabbed each of us by an ear and pulled hard. We both cried in pain and embarrassment as she frog-marched us to the front of the room and ordered us to sit in two chairs facing the class.

We sat. Through my tears, I saw all these strange faces, some wide-eyed, some laughing, especially the boys. Since that day, I always have reckoned chagrin as a worse pain than a punch in the nose. I felt both that day. Miss Ross said Ray and I were bad boys, and that anyone who fought in her kindergarten would suffer for it.

She told Ray and me to pick up our chairs and follow her to the back of the room. She sat Ray in the left corner, facing the wall, and pointed me to the right corner. Everyone else, she said, was going to sing while we thought about how we were not ever going to fight again.

Chairs scuffled. Tittering kids sat down behind us. Playing the piano, Miss Ross warbled "Twinkle-Twinkle, Little Star," a song Mom had taught me and that I ached to sing, so that I might display my excellent voice. Instead, snuffing, I stared at the cracks in the wall.

Dislike of Ray oozed into my cells. For the next decade, he and I fought in classes, in the hallways, in the schoolyard, and on the streets—good training, if irrational, for both of us. I finally whipped him one day within sight of his own yard with a punch that bloodied his nose. After that, he never challenged me again. I never gave him reason. His fists had hurt me enough.

In kindergarten, I learned about pecking order. If you didn't want to be pecked physically, not just by boys but by girls, too, you had to punch, kick, and bite. If you didn't want to be pecked emotionally, that was a different matter. The physical pecking order arranged itself around the aggression of boys. For the emotional, girls and certain boys determined social ranking. Responding to it was far more subtle than the more rewarding physical aggression. I never became good at it.

Soon I learned that the physically or mentally crippled served as victims, as they do among all social animals, to make everyone else feel better. Johnny Nordale was the mayor's son. His father's position should have assured him a revered place in our society of little savages. But he was backward—nice but backward. He was as big as anyone, but awkward. Johnny would punch back if you swatted him, and he harbored a temper without end if you hit him. Word was that he might kill you. We boys kept our distance. Some girls liked to pinch him and run. Johnny struggled to speak. Miss Ross clued him along. But when she wasn't attending to him, we taunted him, mocked how he moved, called him a dummy, and put sand in his paste pot. Worst of all, we pretended he didn't exist, looking through and past him, the invisible boy. He and I shared classes into high school. I regret to say I never had the courage—or even the notion, then—to apologize to him.

In social prestige, Andrea Pratt topped the mountain for the rest of us moppets and urchins. Her father was Judge Harry Pratt, the federal judge, the only real judge in Fairbanks. My mom liked to drop into conversations with neighbors that I played with Andrea. Because my father clerked for a living, I ranked low in kindergarten and thereafter in Fairbanks schools. The top boy among my contemporaries, in kindergarten and for years after, was Bob Burglin. He carried the burden of being the son—God help us all—of a *divorced* woman, a person of great interest and suspicion in a culture where men prevailed. Mrs. Burglin was the exception. She was a handsome, independent woman who distinguished herself by succeeding in her own business, as a public stenographer. Gossip about her ranged from the envious to the salacious, but never to her face. Hypocrisy, I soon saw, oiled small-town life, and as I learned later, is the chief lubricant of civilization.

Mrs. Burglin's station neither elevated nor lowered Bob Burglin in my schoolboy eyes. Bob had his own major talents that ranked him number one among the hens and roosters of the sandbox. He fearlessly kicked, butted, and punched with skill, speed and grace. He had money, real money—coins jingling in his pocket that he spent on candy and pop and ice cream for his friends after school. He was smart and funny. Later, he also proved to be something else we all admired extravagantly, without forethought, something Americans must admire without qualm: Bob was an athlete, not a great one, but good enough.

In kindergarten, I made a friend for life in Alfred Baumeister, a small black-haired boy with the face of a handsome monkey. Alfred was cracking quick in body and mind, a whiz at ABCs and numbers, and a maker of wisecracks. Because he was small, we larger creatures pounced upon him, to show him his place in the sandbox. I quickly learned that if you battled Alfred you reaped in return a tornado of punches, gouges, kicks, scratches and bites, knees in testicles, and thumbs in eyes. I was enough bigger that if I could grab him I might wrestle him to the floor and use my weight to pin him. But our clutched journey from upright to horizontal produced agonies for me akin to wrestling a wildcat. It could be done, but not wisely. Once Alfred and I grasped that we both saw the world as an absurd comedy taken seriously only by hypocrites and buffoons, we became pals, and our friendship has endured for more than sixty years, despite our not seeing one another for long intervals.

At the very bottom of our school pecking order hunkered the Indian, Eskimo, and half-breed children, what few attended school.

(I did not learn until after college that our federal government, through the Department of Interior and its corrupt Bureau of Indian Affairs, had been and still was shipping Native children from their homes all over Alaska, at point of bayonet, as it were, to religious and other schools set up to "civilize" what the rulers among us considered savages. This savage policy created broken families, drunkenness, drug addictions, suicides, homicides, and general animosity.)

My mother frequently warned me and Buzz not to play with or to touch "Natives"—the encompassing term at home and school for the indigenous Alaskans that the white settlers, in the American way, shoved aside and didn't give a damn about unless one could make money off them. Natives, Mom said, were dirty and had diseases. That was frequently true then, just as it was for white children from families with little money, education, or expectations. Ringworm and impetigo, a highly infectious skin condition, adorned both red and white skin. Pink eyes drained pus. Rickets bowed legs. Scurvy caused some children to spit out teeth. Little kids coughed yellow and bloody snot, thanks to tuberculosis, and stopped growing as the disease weeded out the poorest among us and some of the richer too. Teachers inspected us for lice. Nit picking, when I was a boy, was less a metaphor than an experience. A child with a cleft lip or a club foot or any other deformity received extra measures of disdain and ridicule, and not just from schoolmates.

The Native kids not only looked physically different than the rest of us but, due to the poverty that escorted them, they also dressed differently, not in Native clothing, but in hand-me-downs and old, ill-fitting shoes from church charities. Many spoke with accents. Some of us whites had accents from home, too, that school laughter and mockery sanded down in a hurry. The Native children had enunciations deriving from their regional languages, so different from English and European languages. These ways of speaking decorated their speech with clucks, stops, and nasals that we ridiculed. One day after class, when we were about ten, John Johns, an Indian from Fort

Yukon, punched and split my lips for making fun of how he spoke—a beating I deserved, though of course I thought otherwise at the time.

John, like many other Native children, also suffered the burden of an unidiomatic combination of English names—John Johns, Sam Charlie, Betty Susan, Gloria Gloria, and so on—awkward names branded on them by white missionaries and teachers (often the teachers *were* missionaries). We of the ruling class, especially those like me on the hind end of white society, loved making fun of those names. But I changed my ways after a week of split lips imposed on me by John Johns, coming quickly to doubt the wisdom of invoking his wrath again, over anything.

Few Native children stayed with us as we progressed from one class to another. Few entered high school. Fewer yet graduated, even in a territory that bragged about its educational excellence compared, say, to Alabama, Idaho, or other woebegone parts of the Lower 48.

In kindergarten, Miss Ross introduced me to music, which became a great love of my life. Previously, I had heard popular music on KFAR Radio, chiefly swing, a jazz form that still palpitates my heart. In the Church of the Immaculate Conception, I heard choral music coming to me from on high, literally from the choir loft jutting out over the rear one-quarter of that small church, then the only Catholic church in Fairbanks. Yet, until Miss Ross taught me to ting-a-ling a small steel triangle in rhythm with fellow musicians rubbing sticks together or beating on little drums or shaking tambourines or, most prestigious of all, hammering padded sticks on bells, I had no idea that music arose from synchronized human activity. Yes, to define as music the sounds we tadpoles rapped, rattled, and banged would stretch credulity, but to me it equaled the heavenly choirs and chants of the angels that the priests said flocked about God in Heaven.

Our music, with Miss Ross on the piano playing melody with one hand while she conducted with the other, thrilled me and reorganized my brain for eager reception of the musical arts.

Miss Ross was first among several Fairbanks teachers who year after year, advanced my musical knowledge and tastes, leading me to enjoyments that have uplifted me ever since. I utter blessings upon the school system of that time and place for insisting on music being a constant part of the school experience for primitives, small and large.

In Fairbanks, spring arrives in May. Miss Ross and another teacher rigged a celebratory maypole in our kindergarten room as we watched in mystery, suspense, and delight. Classmates more reliable than I fetched and carried as the teachers, with wooden stepladders, attached crepe-paper streamers to the pole's top, alternating white, red, blue, and yellow. The streamers dangled to the floor. Then Miss Ross chose a few of the more sure-footed (I was not among them) to become the first to learn to saunter to music at the maypole, to grasp streamers, skip outward with them, then intertwine joyously in and out and around the pagan pole, on top of which the teachers placed a golden ball, completing the phallic symbolism.

We rehearsed in our room as Miss Ross beat out the rhythms on the piano and other teachers corrected our mistakes of footing and timing. We also learned how to bow, secure the streamers, move, and tip and stow the pole for Main School's outdoor spring festival, to which parents were invited. To say I excelled at maypole dancing would be a lie. I never have excelled in any dancing, an awkward handicap given that dances offered one of the chief weekend amusements in isolated communities all over North America. Still, I managed to tumble along more or less in time with the other children.

Because we kindergartners performed first, we received the full attention of the moms and dads enduring folding chairs or standing behind in the play area in the front of Main School.

Primed with plaudits to dispense upon their posterity and not yet numbed by one student performance after another, the audience lavished us with applause. Mom and neighbor women praised my execution of the maypole as if I were ready for the stage. I basked in their insincerity.

The maypole is disappearing from American life. Today's puritans disapprove of the pole as a pagan symbol. Dancing around it harkens back to debauches in Teutonic forests in the time before the bounty of Christ was spread upon the heathen there, eventually replacing their spring sex festival with Easter's mysteries and with burnings at the stake, in the most Christian-like fashion, of recalcitrant maypole dancers.

That the maypole stood erect and proud in early Twentieth Century Fairbanks I credit to, and forever give thanks to, the isolation of that mining town from the spreading, syrupy uplift of American popular culture.

Thirteen

MY FIRST GRAYLING

It was the Fourth of July, my sixth birthday, a day with no dynamite blasts. No raucous voices could be heard, only a breeze sifting through willows where robins and chickadees chortled: stay away, stay away, this place is mine, this place is mine. The Salcha River's tea-colored water slipped over golden gravels. We had driven onto a large cobblestone bar, where Mom and Dad had spread a canvas and on top of it laid blankets and pillows and boxes containing our picnic potato salad and fried chicken. Brother Buzz, now two and a half, strained against a tether snapped to a harness around his chest and tied to the front bumper of the Plymouth.

It was sunny and hot, and the mosquitoes tolerable. We all smelled sweet with Citronella oil that Mom and Dad lathered on themselves and on Buzz and me. Spot, our black and white mongrel, raced up and down the river's edge indulging in one of his specialties, attempting to catch sandpipers. I urged our dog Spot to catch one but Dad said that would surprise Spot so much he might keel over from the excitement of it.

After arranging the picnic area, Dad donned hip boots. Then he joined two bamboo fly rods as I watched, fascinated. I had seen him fish before, but he had promised me this day that he would teach me to fish. He showed me how he rubbed the rods' male metal ferrules against the side of his nose, to oil them before inserting them carefully and slowly into the female ferrules. He made sure the ringed guides lined up on each of the three pieces. On each rod he seated a small fly reel. From the reels he pulled heavy yellow silk lines, stringing them through the guides. He lifted the lid of a metal tin the shape and size of a kipper can. It contained a clear thick liquid—glycerin, he told me. The transparent leader, he said, was made from the guts of silkworms. The glycerin kept the gut soft and supple. Each leader would loop on the end of a fly line, and each leader had two loops on which to attach the flies.

From his brown duckcloth fishing vest, he removed a fat black leather wallet. It opened like a book to pages of sheepskin covered with white wool. Hooked in the wool, each tied to a short leader with a loop on its end, were fishing flies—black flies with red tails and gray wings called Black Gnats; gray flies called Mosquitoes or Gray Hackles; blue and white flies with silver bodies called Silver Doctors; yellow flies called Yellow Hackles, and many others, page after page. To each leader Dad looped a Silver Doctor at the bottom and a Black Gnat above.

He showed me how to carry the rod: hold it by the cork handle and carry it reel first, with the tip of the rod following behind so it would not get caught in the brush. He picked up his rod and, holding my free hand, we headed for the river. Barefoot, I ouched along.

Dad stowed his rod against a bleached driftwood log. "Watch the swallows," he said. "They're catching bugs on the surface of the water—a good sign. See the little rings on the water? Those are grayling, sipping flies from the surface. That's what we want to see."

We walked to the end of a spit of golden sand. Gently, slowly, he showed me how to turn the rod around, pointing its tip toward the river; how to loosen a little line from the reel, so that I could unhook the fly from where it latched onto a tiny keeper ring above the rod's handle.

"Work some line out," he said, "enough to bend the rod, because it's the line we're casting: The fly follows." Kneeling, he gave me my first casting lesson.

It was frustrating. I tried to throw the rod. Dad corrected me, over and over: thumb on top of the handle, move your wrist only, start high and end high, back and forth. Finally, the line sailed, not far, but far enough. The two flies kissed the water, floated. Excited, I neglected to hold the rod up to slack the line so that the flies would float. When the current tightened the line, the flies skidded across the surface.

Under the Silver Doctor, the water bulged. Dad's hand helped me lift the rod. "Don't jerk it, just lift," he said. The line tightened. A silver blue grayling leaped and thrashed. Laughing and hollering, I jerked the fish onto the shore where it flopped. Mom shouted encouragement. Dad laughed. I wet my pants but felt no embarrassment. In my brain rushed primitive joy and hope. I almost broke the rod as I dove on the poor fish. I shoved it up higher on the bar, felt its struggle. I had no mercy. I wanted it, dearly. It slipped from my fingers, flopped, flipped. Sand coated it. Dad grabbed it, whacked its head against a rock, and handed it to me. In my hand the silver grayling quivered. One big eye looked up. Blood seeped from a gill. Its trembling quit. Its blue iridescence faded. I whooped.

I rushed to present the grayling to my mom. She received me with smiles and praise. It was eight inches long, my first fish. I was hooked forever.

Fourteen

GROUSE HUNTING

At first light, our Plymouth crept forward in low gear along the gravel road, headlights on high. Dad was driving. In the front seat beside him, Mom sipped coffee. A double-barrel shotgun poked up between them. I knelt on the back seat, excited, staring intently down the road looking for shadowy chicken shapes. Buzz stood up so he could see. Coming in through the top of windows opened an inch to keep them from fogging were the cool, ripe fall smells of cottonwoods, aspen, willows and birch, overlain with the tart perfume of juice-filled high-bush cranberries.

The tires crunched along an abandoned stretch of the old meandering, one-lane stage road that ran parallel to the Richardson Highway, both following the milky, glacier-fed Tanana River.

My dad pushed in the clutch, and the car coasted to a stop. On the road ahead, I could just see four or five fool hens pecking gravel. These dark-meat spruce grouse were what we had come for. Dad opened his door slowly, quietly, on hinges that he had oiled the night before. He slid out cradling the shotgun, muzzle ahead of him. My heart raced. I started to speak, but Mom hushed me.

A cock spruce grouse paced nervously. My dad took slow, soft, hunter's steps toward them. He stopped, shouldered the shotgun, and aimed—BANG, BANG! Two grouse fell and flopped. The rest flushed.

Dad quickly ejected the spent shells and reloaded. BANG! A grouse in the air exploded in feathers, crashed. The others dove into the mixed forest. Gray gun smoke drifted into the trees.

I jumped out and scampered to do my job, reaching down to grab the cock, a dark, gray-barred bird with red slashes over his eyes. Blood trickled from a nostril. Holding it by the neck, I snapped my wrist, as Dad had taught me, to wring out what life still throbbed in the rooster. Then I twisted the neck of a hen bird beside it. I felt warmth through their feathers. The birds smelled of spruce. I imagined I could feel them tremble through my palms, but they were dead.

Dad ran down the road and into the brush, retrieving the third bird. We carried them back to the car together, all smiles. Mom chirped happiness. Buzz, laughing, asked to hold one. My dad handed him his bird. Like most birds Dad shot in the air, it was hit in the head and was dead before it crashed to the ground.

Another fall weekend hunt for grouse and ptarmigan had begun, a ritual in our family over the next nine years. Dad also kept a .30-.30 Winchester rifle in the car, in a case between Buzz and me in the back seat, should we see a bull moose. My dad's regular moose hunt would come later, just before river freeze up, when he, Bill Hunter, Ed Clausen, and other friends hunted moose and caribou from a tent camp on the Tanana River flats that they went to by boats.

Hunting and fishing were important to Dad as a way to feed our family. We never had enough money, nor space in our cabin, for a refrigerator. Home freezers didn't exist. Commercial meat lockers were available but we couldn't afford to rent one by ourselves. Dad always tried to shoot the two caribou and one bull moose that the law allowed. He timed his hunt around freeze-up so he could hang the big quarters of meat in our shed, where the cold would preserve them until spring. All we had to do was saw off a frozen roast or steaks in the morning and let it thaw all day for dinner.

Even so, because hack sawing off a steak is hard work in the cold, he and Mom often shared a commercial locker with several other families. In it they stored dressed grouse, ptarmigan, ducks, geese, grayling, salmon, northern pike, whitefish, sheefish, snowshoe rabbits and cuts of moose, caribou, and Dall mountain sheep. Everything was wrapped in thick tan butcher paper, tied with heavy white twine, and labeled in big black letters. The locker meat would feed us not just for the coming winter but also for the following spring and summer, when our shed would be too warm and fly-filled for hanging meat. Mom would tolerate a lot, but she could not stomach flesh that bluebottle flies had trotted on.

My folks also stored heavy white earthenware crocks in our shed. In these were salted slabs of dog (chum) salmon that we snagged and dragged out of the Tanana, the Salcha, the Little Salcha, and other streams and creeks with big treble hooks weighted with lead. This was not an artful form of fishing, but efficient for our purposes.

We ate everything we killed and we killed a lot. We weren't the only ones. Many Fairbanks families faced lean times at the dinner table if they lacked wild fish and game and homegrown and home-canned vegetables. Beef, if it wasn't hamburger or kidneys or tongue or heart, made rare appearances in the de Yonge kitchen, for celebrations only. A canned or smoked ham appeared on holidays. Corned beef arrived on Saint Patrick's Day and lamb at Easter, in deference to my mother. Dad joked, in a way she didn't like, that the best thing about religion was that on certain days you got a day off and you ate good grub. Turkeys imported from Outside graced our table on Thanksgiving and again at Christmas if we already had eaten the geese dad shot. On Sundays, especially in summer and for picnics, a locally grown chicken might decorate our plates.

Dad never hid his disdain for "sports" or "headhunters"—people who killed for fun and for reputation, and not because they had to. He taught Buzz and me that the lowest creature on earth, fit only for digging his own grave and then being put in it, was someone who shoots to see an animal suffer and leaves it to die. Slightly higher on the scale of unworthiness was someone who killed an animal but failed to harvest it all or to harvest it correctly. At the same level stood someone who killed to get a trophy head to stuff and mount on the wall. Among those he especially disliked were "dudes" who came north to kill for an official record—the biggest antlers, usually—and then be photographed and go back Outside to brag about how brave and tough they were to knock down a moose or grizzly bear with a heavy-caliber rifle bullet.

Anyone who can shoot can kill any big animal with a single shot that involves no more danger to him than shooting a cow, Dad would say. As a boy, I never believed that. I read copies of *Outdoor Life* and *Field & Stream*, which then as today connected big-game hunting with personal danger and masculine fitness and excellence. It wasn't until I shot my first moose and caribou that I understood my father was right: killing is easy.

Also ranking high on Harry de Yonge's scale of disdain was the hunter who wouldn't eat wild meat but who would harvest and give the meat away, not to the poor who needed it, but to his betters with whom he wished to curry favor with gifts of caribou tongue (a delicacy) or moose steak (excellent if you have strong jaws). Even now, so many years later, I still embrace my father's attitudes toward those who hunt for trophy, for the thrill of hurting an animal, for the sole purpose of giving meat away to win favors. To visit an office or a home and see a stuffed Alaska brown bear stand in fierce pose in a corner or see the head of a rare African Ibex mountain goat poking out of a wall or a stuffed wolf snarling by a fireplace flashes me with the instant judgment that I am visiting someone devoid of morals, taste, and good sense. Nothing in years of public life ever convinced me otherwise.

The fall of my seventh year my dad taught me how to gut grouse and ptarmigan and how to skin them and keep the flesh in good condition. Once the snows came, he taught me where to hunt for snowshoe rabbits, how to see and understand their trails, and how to set piano wire snares for them. I also learned how to gut the hares, once thawed, without puncturing the bladder or the gall bladder and ruining the meat. I loved nothing more than going out with my dad on a brisk winter morning with new snow, pulling a toboggan on which Dad had strapped our snowshoes. The trapping lessons I applied later when, from nine onward, I ran my own snare line for rabbits. On the toboggan, Dad also lashed a box containing a flashlight, extra flashlight bulbs, candles, waterproof matches, tea bags, tin cups, a small pot for melting snow and boiling the water, and our lunch, which was always something we could eat even if it was frozen. On top, he tied a sheath holding a loaded .22 Remington pump, a rifle I still keep. The fat and white plumber's candles he cut into short lengths. If you know how, and he taught me, you can kindle a campfire quickly by stacking dry twigs and branches over a candle set in a small hole in the snow. Each of us also carried, "just in case," a couple of pieces of candle and waterproof matches in a secure coat pocket. Dad carried the flashlight batteries in his inside pockets. The batteries didn't work well or long when they were cold. Sometimes we'd warm them under our armpits.

We each carried a multi-blade pocketknife and a small hunting knife in sheaths on our belts. The knives had sharp, sharp blades. He taught me how to sharpen the blades. We each carried sugar cubes to suck if we felt tired and a few Band-Aids for the inevitable small cuts.

From first snow to spring melt, if the snowshoe hares were plentiful—their numbers went up and down—we'd bring home a half-dozen or more rabbits from a day's rounds on the snare line. We never ran the line during bitter cold. It was painful and potentially dangerous. A fall or sprained ankle at forty below could mean death. It didn't matter if we waited a couple of frigid weekends. The snared rabbits remained frozen until we picked them up.

In teaching me and my little brother how to shoot the .410 shotgun and the .22 rifle, Dad enforced rigorous firearm safety. Buzz once pulled the trigger on the .22 that I had laid on a table but had failed to empty. The rifle spat. The bullet made a hole in the wall next to my belly. For a year, Buzz and I were forbidden from touching a weapon—and we didn't, Dad's moral power was so strong over us.

By age ten, I was going on trips with my dad and his friends and their sons hunting for caribou and moose. Mom never hunted. Sometimes she shot targets with the .22. Buzz never did hunt big game because he was three years younger than I. By the time Buzz was ten, Dad was sixty-seven and had crippled himself by breaking a hip falling on ice.

My father's hip healed some, but mended poorly. His leg shrank, putting his toes about an inch off the ground when he was standing, and his heel was even higher. Having spent much of his free time hunting and fishing, Dad now found himself unable to walk far or fast, unable to slog through soggy tundra after caribou or trudge bottom lands after moose. He no longer could lift heavy weights. Leaning on his cane, he could chop with a hatchet but not swing an axe. He dared not climb a ladder at home, where the roof and gutters required constant repair, or at work, where in the storage areas of the N.C. hardware some bins were thirty feet above the floor and clerks accessed them via wooden ladders permanently affixed on rollers that slid along the walls. He struggled putting on a shoe on that weak leg, muttering choice Dutch curses.

His fall on the ice not only broke his hip but loosed old age upon him.

He still let me row him summer evenings out to weed patches at Harding and Birch lakes to cast for pike. But getting in and out of a boat was difficult. He tried to fly-fish for grayling without wading, but that didn't work. He caned about open sandbars, confined to areas too hammered by other anglers to harbor the big bronze-backed grayling that he loved to lure to the surface with floating flies.

Frustration forced him to put his rods aside and become a cheerleader for me. I fished with the fervor he felt.

Our old Plymouth, with its clutch and floor-mounted shift, was difficult for him to drive, but he managed. So we continued the family tradition in the fall of rising well before dawn and rolling out to our grouse-hunting roads, where we cruised slowly, looking for the dark forms in the dawn light. But now I had became the chief hunter, with the .410 shotgun in my hands in the back seat, carefully easing the car door open as the Plymouth coasted to a halt, smelling the inflow of cool fall air scented with decaying leaves and ripe berries, stepping out slowly to load the little shotgun, snap its double barrels shut, and begin the slow stalk forward to get within range of fool hens, willow grouse, pintail grouse, willow, and sometimes rock ptarmigan. When I pulled the first trigger and then the second and the gun barked once, twice, and two or more birds slammed to earth, fluttering, dying, I never thought, never wondered what the old man driving the car might be feeling.

When my brother and I picked up the birds and returned to the car, Dad and Mom would smile and nod, welcoming us back as young heroes. This was as close to exaltation as I ever would feel, a boy on the edges of a vast wilderness still long on animals and fish and short on people.

Fifteen

WAR

Smudged ground-level windows let in the dim glow of streetlights that softened shadows in the chilly basement of the Church of the Immaculate Conception, next to the hospital, across the Chena River from downtown. From the ceiling dangled two light bulbs. Under one, in a pool of yellow light, a dozen Sunday school kids, me among them, squirmed on metal fold-up chairs.

From a lectern, a Jesuit priest, Father Charles I think, a bent, skinny man with stubble of gray whiskers, wattles cascading from his Adam's apple, and dandruff snowing on his black stole, led us through catechisms filled with colored drawings. Walking among us, Sister Angelica, tall and quick in black-and-white nun's garb, tapped the flat of a metal-edged ruler against her palm, to cue us to stay awake.

She rendered a simple stimulus to those who nodded off—a sharp rap with the ruler's edge against the back of the neck. It stung like a bee.

For a second offense, she'd command, "Hands out with your palms up!"

WHAP! The ruler's edge reddened your palm with fire. You didn't want to cry, not aloud. Crying irritated the hell out of Father Charles. At his nod, Sister disbursed a second blow.

A third transgression—later confessed at length to the same priest—caused you to be wrenched to your feet, with Sister Angelica's hand twisting your ear and dragging you to a distant dark corner to stand while she whapped your butt until she felt better. Word spread among us seven-year-olds studying for First Communion that in those dank corners hunched huge spiders the color of dead flesh, which scampered down the walls to embrace you and suck your throat. When asked about these reports, our teacher did not disabuse us of the existence of these terrible spiders. Whatever happened to bad boys and girls, he said, they deserved. To find out about what goes on in the corners of the dark basement, go stand there yourselves. No one volunteered.

That December morning had been so cold and dark my mom had walked me from our cabin up Wendell to Lacey Street. Where Lacey ended at the Chena River, trucks dumped ashes over the bank onto the river ice. I'm not sure where the ashes came from. They probably came from the N.C. powerhouse a few blocks away because the tan ashes had hard, black cinders in them. In the spring, ice breakup and high water were supposed to carry the ashes out of town, but they never did. The ash heap kept growing wider and wider, jutting farther and farther out into the river. Residents dumped bottles and cans and other garbage onto this peninsula so that in summer, barefoot boys running on it could discover how glass shards and the lids of rusty cans sliced your feet.

Through the snow atop the ash heap, my mom and others had worn a slippery winter path down to the frozen river. The path angled across the Chena to a steep bank on the other side. There, ice glazed the upward sweep of the path, and good citizens had hacked steps into the ice so that you could climb really high before you slipped and tumbled backwards.

Once on top of the far riverbank, bearing left, you traipsed across a field where, in the summer, nuns cultivated a truck garden. The path forked there. One path led to a door that opened into an odd-smelling area of Saint Joseph's Hospital where the nuns lived.

The other path led to a side door of the church that opened into a hallway that smelled of incense, candles, and bleach. On the left, stairs rose to the sacristy, where priests and altar boys vested for mass. Off the hallway were the Father Superior's office and offices shared by other Jesuits, a communal room where they smoked and read books and newspapers and holy texts, and their dining room adjoining a kitchen. Along the way, stairs descended to the basement where little Catholics studied the sacred texts and where the big ghostly spiders lived.

This particular morning, my mother had deposited me in the church basement with fifteen or so other future communicants, some of them my second-grade classmates from Main School.

Experience had primed me for a long and dreary morning, but one not without some interest, because we would begin examining the pages illustrating what happened to good Catholic children who made an earnest and sin-free First Communion; what happened to depraved Catholic children who did not; what happened to children who were dangerous and despised Protestants or, worse, Buddhists, Hindus, followers of Muhammad, other heathens and infidels, and the worst of all—Jews, the Jesus killers. Mom and I had read these pages together, and she had drilled me on their content so that she would not hear from the priest that I hadn't done my homework.

The catechism book showed Catholic children upon First Communion with their own guardian angels. In the illustrations, the children were all white, of course, like Dick and Jane in our schoolbooks. Most had blond or red hair, with a few brunettes thrown in. The guardian angels all looked like sissy boys, pure white, with golden haloes, blond tresses flowing over white gowns down almost to their bare feet. From their robes, great white-feathered wings protruded. The wings, even when folded, curved higher than their shoulders and the tips tickled their heels. When flying, guardian angels had enormous wingspans. That made sense to me. Those wings had to carry aloft an angel almost the size of a woman. Some guardian angels hefted enormous fiery swords brandished to drive devils away from good little Catholic boys and girls.

Cherubs also adorned these illustrations. Cherubs flew on quite tiny wings sticking out of their baby backs. Having become a maker and flier of balsa-wood gliders, thanks to lessons from my dad, and thus one who appreciated the relationship among wings, fuselage and lift, I reckoned that if they weren't angels, Cherubs would look black and blue from crash landings.

The Catholic children with guardian angels split into three groups. The smallest group lived lives pure from sin. They obeyed the Ten Commandments, not even committing adultery, whatever that was, or coveting their neighbors' wives. They didn't lie. They didn't cheat. They didn't steal. I decided that they did not go to school in Fairbanks, either. Every kid I knew lied, if only in self-defense. Certainly I did. To each other, but never to our parents or teachers, we confessed to cheating on school lessons. We thanked the Lord there was no commandment against copying your neighbor's papers in school.

In the catechism, if they suffered the inconvenience of dying, causes and methods unspecified, the pure children levitated through the clouds, hand in hand with their guardian angels to Heaven, where Jesus awaited them with a rapturous smile and outstretched arms. Behind him were the Virgin Mary, the apostles, and other saints in a vast, joyful welcoming committee.

In the sternest way possible, Father Charles said these were the good children that we should become. But, he said sadly, as Sister and he knew only too well, more likely we all would become more like the second set of children with guardian angels—sinners who repented, who rejoiced in being forgiven and, when they died, would stop first in Purgatory for thousands upon thousands of years of scorching. Fire and heat and smoke, he said, pointing to the illustration of Purgatory, would bleach your souls of sins' black stains.

Purgatory fascinated us. The bright-colored illustration showed children and adults with great smiles on their faces being toasted over bonfires while angels blew long trumpets and strummed little harps. I had seen neither instrument nor heard them but, according to Father Charles, the Purgatorial music promised that the folks in Purgatory, after a trifling ten thousand years of roasting, would join hands with angels who at last would hoist them to Heaven. Sure enough, in one corner of the picture of Purgatory, clean souls with musical notes flying out of their mouths rose in hand with big, sword-carrying angels up to Jesus, Mary, Joseph, the apostles, and all the saints.

The third group of Catholics included many little kids. Father Charles said that they had died before they had a chance on earth to purge themselves of sins, especially Original Sin, which stained us all the moment we were born. (I never understood what Original Sin was, and still don't, I regret to say.) These innocents carried Original Sin as stain on their souls and, because they died before they could understand sin, the angels whisked them off to Limbo. We knew little kids died all the time, sometimes in our own families, or down the street in the homes of kids we played with. So I studied Limbo with ardor. It seemed to be a dull place, a field of clouds, devoid of anything other than little kids floating around not knowing that forever and forever, according to Father Charles, they would be deprived of the joy of seeing Jesus. As one easily bored, I supposed the punishing tedium of Limbo to be far worse than the crime of dying innocent of the knowledge of sin, not that I was in danger of that.

The most interesting thing of all happened to the Catholic kids who, after First Communion, sinned and died before they could confess to a priest and be forgiven: Hell awaited them with leaping red flames, dirty black smoke, orange lava, steam, and the upturned, howling faces of children and men and women being boiled, broiled, stabbed, forked, skewered, pinched, gutted and flayed by devils of many sizes and shapes whose faces reflected professional devotion to their work. According to Father Charles, Satan and other devils also suffered these intense agonies, though it appeared from the pictures that they were having a good time.

"No getting out of Hell, never!" Father Charles shouted. "Forever in Hell! Not one moment without terrible pain and the most terrible pain of all! Knowing that as a sinner you rejected God—the true God!"

Hell might be a wonder-filled place to visit, but you wouldn't want to live there.

Some of us in catechism class shuddered and looked around the room at the others, knowing deep in our souls that likely we would end up in Hell. If not me, I assumed, then Bobby over there, who started fights, and Ronnie, who always wanted to drop his trousers if you would drop yours, so we could play with each other's thingy, or Mary up front, who would steal your pencil and eraser or anything else you didn't watch when she was around.

The bad Catholic kids formed a not insignificant queue into the fire and brimstone, which Father Charles said smelled like the smoke from a sulfur match. But they were far from alone. Indeed, in the picture, mobs of other children dwarfed the Catholic contribution to Hell—the children of other religions. Father Charles said they were being brought up as sinners, and once they are as old as you are, they have reason, and sooner or later have contact with the true, holy, one-and-only Catholic Church. Yet, he sniffed sadly, they don't use their reason, they don't abandon the false doctrines taught them by their mothers and fathers, and so, sooner or later, whether they die as children or die as old men and women, they will be collected by the devils and driven into Hell.

I confess that for many years this thought of all non-Catholics going to Hell comforted me, especially when I found many of them to be more handsome than I, more sprightly and agile, just as smart or smarter, a lot richer, and in all, people to envy, except for their final descents into the Pit.

It was a religious truth of my boyhood that the other Catholics, the kind who didn't worship the Pope and didn't obey him, probably would end up in the sulfurous fires. Such other brands of Catholics existed right in our church. Thanks to the gold rush, Fairbanks had lots of "itches" and "vices" and "enskys" and "als" in its mix of last names, but no Greek, Russian Orthodox, Marion, or other non-Roman Catholic churches. Many of these folk attended our church. Mom sniffed that they had not been brought up in the true faith but came from a branch of Catholicism close enough to allow them to enter our sacred portals. Sometimes she added that one of the great benefits of being born pure Irish as she was, and half-Irish as my brother and I were, was that the true religion coursed in your blood; it was right inside you, inborn, a ticket straight into Heaven if you had the brains to follow the directions printed upon it.

On this December day, Father Superior strode in just as Bobby Burglin and I were savoring the prospect of telling Alfred Baumeister and our other Protestant and heathen pals about where they were going when they died. Rosary beads hanging from his waist clacked as he paced to Father Charles and whispered into his ear. Father Charles beckoned Sister Angelica, who swished over to join them. Her head bent toward theirs. Then she looked over her shoulder at us.

Class is over, Father Charles said. Your parents will pick you up soon. Stay here. Stay in your seats. We'll return soon.

The three of them left hurriedly. We burst out of our chairs, laughing. Hardly had our joy pulsed before Sister Angelica reappeared and rulered us back into submission. Soon, one parent after another entered to gather up offspring. When Mom arrived, I saw that she was upset. This warned me not to spark her anger. Her hands far exceeded Sister Angelica's in speed and accuracy delivering a stinging slap.

Mom bundled me for the trudge home in the day glow of the cold and dreary fog. A terrible thing has happened, she said. The Japs have attacked Pearl Harbor. War! I had no idea what Japs were or where Pearl Harbor was. Already I was reading War Comics and Wings, in which brave Englishmen and American volunteers in Spitfires and Hurricanes shot scar-faced Nazi pilots out of the air. I understood war to be a mechanized sport the good guys always won.

Mom and I hurried across the sisters' snowy garden, slid on our fannies down the path onto the Chena, and crossed the river with others. In the half-light of the freezing gloom, no one stopped to talk—a warning that whoever the Japs were and wherever Pearl Harbor was, the attack was scary and bad. I trotted to keep up, my hand in Mom's, mitten to mitten, puffs of breath frosting in the air behind us.

Once Mom and I navigated the ash heap and turned onto Wendell, I noticed that all the houses were lit up. This was unusual. Electricity was very dear and on a Sunday in 1941, a day of rest, people rose late and then would not show lights until night fell in the early afternoon.

In the front room at home, my dad sat in a straight chair close to our big Zenith radio. Brother Buzz played on the floor with Spot. On winter evenings, life in our house revolved about the radio, with its emerald and amber dials and knobs that eased thin blue and red pointers around the dials. To see Dad with his ear plastered to the radio in the middle of the day signaled that something big was happening.

"Most of our navy's been sunk," he told Mom. "The little yellow bastards!" I didn't know what that meant.

Mom was full of worries. "Will they come here?" Dad shrugged. After lunch, Mom cleared the kitchen table, and Dad laid out his rifles—the Remington pump .22, the lever-action Winchester .30-.30, the bolt-action Remington .30-.06, all with open sights. He set out his cleaning tools and Hoppe's Gun Oil with its wonderful smell. He stacked boxes of cartridges on the table. On an old envelope, he marked how many cartridges he had for each rifle.

"I'll buy more tomorrow at the store," he said. "There'll be a run on them. I'll go in early."

While he cleaned the rifles, the neighbors dropped by. Everyone talked about the Japs, the sons of bitches, about how to hold them off. Mother and the women talked about supplies of beans and flour and canned meat and hoarders. The men drank short shots of my dad's rye whiskey. Mom served coffee and tea and blueberry wine that she and Dad had made in crocks the previous fall in the shed. Bored, Buzz and I fussed. We were shushed. When something new came in over the radio, everyone rushed to the Zenith.

After dinner, he and Mom talked over coffee in the kitchen. "Got to get some dry food ready, Eva," he said, "in case we have to get out of here if the Japs come." Mom started to sniffle. "We can't leave before summer, Harry, in the cold, with the kids. Where could we go that they wouldn't find us?"

"You're right," he said. "I guess they know they can't come in the winter. I hope so. But you don't know. If they come before breakup, I don't know. We'll just have to shoot them in the streets, I guess."

Mom wept.

Buzz and I listened from our bed on the couch across the front room from the radio. Mom and Dad came in, turned the radio up, and listened. Now and then, Dad sat on a stool before the radio and carefully, moving the dial ever so slowly, through the crackles and pops of static and sometimes the sound of high, tinny voices far, far away, hunted for news broadcasts. Being so close to Russia, he found loud voices in what he said was Russian. Sometimes, but not often, with a list of frequencies he had written down, he'd find a clear broadcast from Radio Moscow in English or a newscast from London or Chicago. We listened intently. The radio talk didn't make much sense to me. But I knew something important was happening. War. The word sounded heavy.

I drifted off to sleep thinking of Japs. Mom said they had slanted eyes and yellow skin and walked around in bathrobes. I dreamed of devils prodding Japs into Hell, with pitchforks pushed up under their bathrobes, jabbing them into the flames and smoke along with bunches of Baptists like the Davis family, which lived a couple of blocks away over on Second Avenue near Clay Street. Mr. Davis ran the Baptist church. He would go to Hell in a blue suit and white shirt and black tie with his black shoes split where his little toes bulged. He wore such clothes all the time, I knew, because I played with Geraldine Davis and her brother, Stanley, in their home, and had seen him.

I knew Geraldine and Stanley wouldn't like it in Hell, especially when it would be filled with Japs. But what could I do? The answer to that was the same answer to many questions that arose later in life—nothing.

Sixteen

AN END TO INNOCENCE

A month before I turned eight, my mother rented me to Mr. Jacobs, the music teacher, who each summer planted and tended a big commercial garden where Eighth Avenue ran into Lacey Street at the southern edge of town. Beyond, out in the woods, the Army was building Ladd Field for the Army Air Corps to defend us against the Japanese.

One June morning after breakfast, Mom walked me out to Jacobs' place. I walked my bicycle along. Mr. Jacobs was a lean, gray-haired man who wore a greasy tan cap with the earflaps down, though the sun burned down on us and the temperature already was in the seventies.

Obey him, she said, smiling serenely and rubbing the back of my head. Then she left.

Jacobs showed me a cabbage patch where already, thanks to the intense, prolonged sun of high summer, the cabbage plants grew higher than my knees. He carried an empty one-pound Hills Brothers coffee can.

"Here's what you're looking for," he said. He knelt, patted the earth for me to kneel beside him, and rolled back cabbage leaves until he spotted our prey, a green worm on the underside of a leaf. "Cutworm," he said. "Pluck it off. Put it in the can."

I hesitated.

"Go ahead, pluck it off. You get ten cents an hour and one cent for every one of these you find. You work hard, you can make fifty cents an hour."

That was a lot of money. But it sounded like a lot of worms. I still hesitated.

"Damn it!" He grabbed my right hand. "Take the worm, dump it in the can!" He forced my fingers to the worm, which sensing trouble, began to hump away. "Get him before he's gone, boy!" This time he shoved my fingers onto the worm. It felt rubbery, just before it squished. I jerked back. He clouted me behind the ear. "You'll do it or else!"

I knew what a clout meant. Slobbering, I moved with him to the next plant. We repeated the process. Two worms. I tweezed them with shaking fingers into the can, where they rolled and twisted around, a posture that years later I recognized as the common posture of human beings. "Two cents worth," Mr. Jacobs said. "Work until I come to get you."

He went away, but not far, to hoe and water. He watched me as I shuffled on my knees along the row of cabbages. There seemed to be a thousand cabbages. I was a lardy little kid, no hat, wearing overalls, tee shirt and tennis shoes. Soon, under the relentless sun, sweat beaded my skin. Worms plunked into the can. Welcome to the fabled world of work, Jackie.

I hated cabbage-worming. I hated getting up every morning at six, to pedal out to this tyrant's vegetable empire, to do whatever he commanded: hoe, rake, worm, and weed.

I never saw any money. Each noon when it was time to go home, Mr. Jacobs recorded my time and worm harvest, if one existed, into a ledger book. I departed with alacrity, free for another half-day. I worked five mornings a week. At quitting time each Friday, Mr. Jacobs would hand me a sealed envelope, addressed to my mother. It contained a check for my services, as much as eight dollars if the cabbage-worm harvest had been good. I know the amount because I opened the envelope the first time and caught a clout from my mom for opening her private mail. She took the money, a major contribution to the family finances at a time when my dad earned one hundred dollars a month at the N.C.

Being an ignorant boy, I felt it unjust that not a cent fell into my palm. In my mind's oven, a half-baked thought rose, later to emerge as a glorious final loaf when I hawked newspapers: keep some of the dough for yourself.

In Mr. Jacobs' garden, I turned crisp under the sun. As part of a subarctic desert, in summer's long hours of daylight, Fairbanks temperatures often jump into the eighties, sometimes into the nineties. I had to worm and weed on my knees in the dirt. My back ached. Mosquitoes and moose flies tormented. Mr. Jacobs, if he thought I was not worming with fervor, would pinch my ear to refocus my attention to the task at hand.

Then, one morning, I rebelled. I refused to go to work. Mom, furious, ordered me to trot down to the willows by the river to cut and fetch her a switch so she could whip my backside. I refused to do that, too.

For the first time, fear of the pains my mom could and would inflict failed to make me obey. In one of the epiphanies of my youth, I discovered that whether moved by my dad's Dutch genes for stubbornness or by my mom's Irish genes for rebellion, by God I would not submit, I would not cut my own switch.

Mom pulled me by the ear and frog-marched me down to the willows, a knife swinging in her other hand.

"Cut a switch!" she ordered, eyes blazing.

Blubbering, I shook my head: "No, no, NO!"

She cut a big switch and with motherly love whipped my bare calves. I just stared up at her, bawling, still shaking my head.

That further infuriated her. The lashes rained down on me. I broke and ran into the willows, where I burrowed into hiding. At first, she shouted the details of what she was going to do to me when I came out. After a half-hour or so, she calmed down and began begging me to come forth. I intended to stay where I was until Dad showed up for dinner. At last she left, crying herself, headdown.

By then, mosquitoes had drained a quart of blood from me. I took off through the willows on trails leading toward town. By noon, at the playground, I was exhausted. Even so, I waited and waited and waited until that evening when I saw my father approaching on foot on Wendell, heading home for dinner. I fell in with him. We went inside. My mother stared at me for a second, appraised my father's face, and decided, I think, that I had said nothing to him about our little dustup. She said nothing.

After that, though she still switched me to punish disobedience and relieve her anger, she never again inflicted pain to compel me to work. Instead, she reverted to verbal tirades which, like most boys, I learned to ignore. There is a lot of wisdom and human experience condensed in the little saying about sticks, stones, and bones.

The Cushman Street Bridge, above, was the only span across the Chena River in Fairbanks when I boomed forth into the world in 1934 at Saint Joseph's Hospital, on the right. As a boy, I learned a lot about good and evil at the Church of the Immaculate Conception, center, now a historical landmark. Shortly after my birth, at left, being held in my father's arms in front of our cabin on Wendell Avenue, my expression is questioning—as I came to be through most of my life.

ABOVE: On a deceptively peaceful summer afternoon shortly after the start of World War II, the business and cultural center of Fairbanks is seen along Second Avenue. Conveniently, the Whore Line, as it was called, was only three blocks away.

RIGHT: In his later years, my maternal grandfather, Dan Delaney, stood for a formal portrait wearing knee-high leggings from his days as a gold-rush stampeder. Delaney was a first-generation Irish-American who passed a lot of his hard-headedness to me. He was a tough, hard-working Mick who was willing to march over high mountains and ford wide rivers in search for gold. In his prime, Grandpa Delaney was a miner, a farmer, and a carpenter. According to my mother, Grandpa rarely walked away from a fist-fight that he could lend a hand to.

LEFT: My maternal grandma, Mary McDonough Delaney, stared a bit wide-eyed for a picture, taken about the time she married Dan Delaney in 1893. Her portrait hints at the fortitude she showed later en route to the Klondike, climbing Chilkoot Pass with a pack on her back and her young son, Finian, holding her hand. ABOVE: My mom, Eva Marie Delaney, was photographed in the 1920s about the time my dad, Harry de Yonge, made her acquaintance with a clever line on Market Street in San Francisco. By then, the Delaneys had moved to San Francisco from Fairbanks, having given up their quest for gold due to bad luck, a family tragedy (Finian's disappearance), ill health, and lack of money.

LEFT: My mom stands in the doorway of the shed my dad tacked onto our cabin. This photograph appears to have been taken in the fall when our family worked in the shed putting up barrels of salted dog and king salmon, preparing casks of blueberries for wine-making, washing low-bush cranberries (lingonberries), and hanging up freshly killed fish and game.

ABOVE: My mom, my aunt "Lou" (Louise O'Byrne), and my dad pose for a photograph in front of our family cabin on Wendell Avenue. Aunt Lou and a few friends were among the first civilians to drive to Fairbanks over the new Alaska-Canada Highway. In this photo, Aunt Lou and my mother appear to be tolerating one another—for a change.

Wiley Post, at right, the world-renowned aviator, comes ashore at Fairbanks after landing on the Chena River on August 14, 1935. Post and his sidekick, Will Rogers, were on their way around the world, trying to set a new speed record. Rogers, then America's favorite newspaper columnist, talks with Post on the wing of the *Aurora Borealis,* above. According to de Yonge family lore, Rogers held in his arms a squalling one-year-old, me, after coming ashore to meet scores of Fairbanks residents who turned out to see the famous pair. The next day, the two men died when their plane crashed into the tundra near Barrow on Alaska's north coast.

The three orphaned bear cubs, above, were left with Dad by Charlie "Catcher's Mitt" Cook, who had discovered the cubs after killing the sow. I don't know what happened to the cubs, but I suspect they were eaten. Moments after this photo was taken, this trio escaped from the box, and one of them bit me as I grabbed for it. Thus I learned to forbear bears. That's Buzz and me in the photo below making the best of winter.

Every spring, "breakup" on the Chena River, above, attracted crowds waiting to see if the ice would destroy the Cushman Street Bridge and—more important—to learn who would win the Chena Ice Pool, a game to guess when the ice would "go out." The winning time was established when a pylon on the ice, tethered to a clock onshore, moved far enough to break the connection and stop the clock. Those who guessed the correct day, hour, and minute shared thousands of dollars in prizes. Breakup also brought flooding, seen below in a photograph of Samson Hardware and other buildings across the river from the N.C. Company store and powerhouse.

A common sign of spring on Wendell Avenue was flooding in our neighborhood. My dad built the two cabins on the right, above, which my mom rented out and managed. One of our renters, Joe Heffren, approaches in his power boat on his way to work. Buzz and I are in our spring duds, which included waders.

ABOVE: Our family was sailing north on the *SS Denali* of the Alaska Steamship Line, in the fall of 1939 when we witnessed a pod of orca "killer" whales attack and tear apart a giant gray whale. In a stateroom like the one above, my mother, brother, and I endured horrible seasickness as we sailed through a storm while crossing the Gulf of Alaska to Valdez. RIGHT: My dad, tending to my brother and me, was a former sailor and the only passenger on board who did not succumb to seasickness.

LEFT: Dad, me, Buzz, and my mom rest on the running board of the 1932 Plymouth that carried us wherever a road existed in central Alaska. We were parked on a gravel bar of the Salcha River, where we fly-fished for grayling.

ABOVE: My brother and I pose with shotguns and ptarmigan shot on one of the many domed hills north of Fairbanks. I am holding a double-barrel .410 that I hunted with from the time I was six. My brother holds a 12-gauge pump that at that age he could barely lift, much less shoot. I still own the 12-guage.

LEFT: For a formal class photograph, Miss Brown stands with her first-grade class in the spring of 1941 on the steps of Main School. I am the towheaded fellow in the middle of the top row. Bobby Burglin is on my right. My lifelong friend, Al Baumeister, is in the front row, second from the right. I can still name about half of these urchins though I sometimes forget my own name. A generation of Fairbanks kids learned reading, writing, and arithmetic and other subjects at Main School, a wonderful example of 1930s architecture. The school still stands, housing city offices. In my time, kindergarten and primary grades attended classes in the basement and on the first floor, while high-school classes were situated on the top floor.

ABOVE: A major Fairbanks landmark and place to warm up on the way to school was the Federal Building with its federal courts, government agencies, and a post office that was always busy in an era predating home delivery of mail. The triangular patch of ground in the foreground, left, offered an early place to play marbles each spring when sunlight reflecting from the building melted snow there quickly.

LEFT: With his ever-present pipe, top photo, Dad provides the rowing power on a summer day at Harding Lake. We loved the lake. Each summer, it offered the best vacation a boy could have—swimming, fishing, boating, canoeing, and other adventures. My brother and I learned to swim here, experienced the pain of sunburns, and discovered that moose flies could bite through anybody's hide. Roadside camping, bottom photo, was one of our favorite outings, too. With me is Mary Hunter, my constant baby-sitter. That's my dad in the background.

ABOVE: The U.S. Army parades along First Avenue during the March Ice Festival. In 1941, a handful of military personnel were stationed in and near Fairbanks. A year later, the Army and Army Air Corps, as the air force was known then, flooded the area with young Americans as part of the buildup for World War II. Later, they were joined by Russian pilots, crews, and maintenance personnel who picked up U.S. military aircraft in Fairbanks as part of the lend-lease program

ГРАФИК
ДВИЖЕНИЯ САМОЛЕТОВ
ТИП
ПРИБЫЛО
В РАБОТЕ
ГОТОВЫЕ

LEFT: Soviet pilots at their Ladd Field headquarters, top, prepared to fly lend-lease fighter planes and light bombers across Alaska to the Soviet Union and finally to the war fronts where the Russians fought the Germans and their allies. During the war years, about 8,000 U.S.-built planes flown by American pilots arrived at Ladd Field, where they were transferred to the Russians. Off duty, bottom, the Soviet pilots enjoyed collecting pinups. I was told that pinups were frowned upon by Joe Stalin but that the pilots smuggled them home anyway along with cigarettes, nylon stockings, and other decadent American consumer goods.

ABOVE: Among the many rites of passage for boys on the edge of the frontier, nothing ranked higher than watching and betting on fierce fights between other boys. These fights offered little in the way of finesse but much in the way of punching, kicking, gouging, biting, and other skills necessary for survival. The chief formal rule was: don't kill your opponent. Eye-gouging was considered impolite but sometimes necessary.

In my guise as a high-school sophomore, insouciant in the Fairbanks high style of gloomy youths of the day, I try to look worldly standing before the new 1948 Plymouth my parents bought in anticipation of departing Fairbanks forever. We drove away from Fairbanks just a few weeks after school ended in May that year, 1950.

Seventeen

MRS. FORD

Hulda Ford had been a sporting girl during the Nome Gold Rush, had married a rich man there, took him for all he was worth, brought the money to Fairbanks where she bought up half the town, then went cuckoo with guilt.

Another story was that she'd stampeded to Nome with her husband, a lawyer crooked as a pig's tail, who made it big there, then high-tailed it out of town with a sporting girl because the whore's pimp was going to shoot him. His faithful wife, Hulda, wracked with love and grief, sold out and lugged her Double Eagles to Fairbanks, where she bought up half the town. But the evils of drink possessed her, and look at her now, a rich derelict.

Yet another version of her life story was that she really was a High Yellow from New Orleans who passed herself off as white and when her banker-husband found out, he committed suicide in Nome. She inherited his poke and all the Double Eagles he'd stashed away. A real looker then, Hulda had arrived in Fairbanks shortly after Captain Barnette, the town's founder, looted his own bank and skedaddled to Hollywood with the deposits. She bought the properties of all the people Barnette had ruined, pennies on the dollar. But she liked dope, and blew her brains out her ears snorting cocaine in those days when you could buy it in the drug store.

I heard many theories. Hulda Ford was the name she used on legal documents in Fairbanks, and her name appeared on a lot of them—deeds, bank accounts, and safety deposit box records. But everyone called her "Mrs. Ford."

I first saw Mrs. Ford one summer when I was little. In the middle of the wooden sidewalk in downtown Fairbanks, a mound of clothes advanced toward my mom and me. It looked like a stemless brown mushroom sliding along. It had arms but no legs I could see. A skirt of dirty brown fabric skittered across the sidewalk. Little eyes semi-circled with yellowish white eyebrows and surrounded by bloodshot whites peered from under what looked like a welcome mat. As the apparition neared, smudgy cheeks patched with sparse white whiskers showed. Arms sticking out from under an oilskin cape showed hands in white cotton gloves with the fingers cut off. White threads dangled from the cuts. Her fingers displayed long, curled, blackish fingernails.

Mom squeezed my hand and inched us toward the edge of the sidewalk next to the unpaved, dusty First Avenue in front of Fritz's Lunch, a place my mother loved because of the liverwurst sandwiches Fritz built with an outburst of German. I hated the place because it was narrow, dark, and hot and smelled of frying sausages and onions. The wooden floor rolled up and down. The counter rolled up and down. Fritz wore a towering white cook's hat that terrified me. But now, to get out of the way of this strange creature approaching, I would gladly brave Fritz and his trolls' den. Mom pulled me to her and stopped. The hump of clothes ambled up.

"Hello, Mrs. Ford," my mother said.

The pile kept moving. It kept saying, "I remember, I remember, I remember," in a voice that gurgled like rain through a down spout. I smelled vinegar and old pee mixed with baby shit and mildew. It hung in the air, heavy, oily, palpable. I tried to spit. The stench lay on my tongue.

"That's the richest lady in Fairbanks," my mother said in a tone of admiration as we resumed walking. She waved at a false-fronted, derelict building across the street with high windows filled with cobwebs. She owns that and that and that, Mom said, pointing as we walked along. Later, after I began making my own way around town with other boys, when we looked at one of the many abandoned buildings or houses, I'd say, being Mr. Know-It-All already, Mrs. Ford owns that and that and that. Chances were I wasn't wrong.

My mom and other mothers would say: If you don't stop bothering me, I'm going to turn you over to Mrs. Ford so that she can cook you for dinner. I believed that. I'd seen "Snow White." I knew what witches could do. My chums and I figured Mrs. Ford was a witch, judging by her dress, demeanor, and stink.

The old woman provoked envy. Most of us were poor, not in the sense of starving poverty, but in the sense poverty would grind us down if something happened to the man in the house, the wage-earner, or to a divorced or abandoned mother working for slave wages. The adults talked about Mrs. Ford all the time, and the main subject was her money. How they wished they had it. They'd kiss Fairbanks good-bye.

Mrs. Ford walked the streets night and day. Sometimes, on winter days, when the cold cut into you like fangs even though you wore heavy parkas and mittens and scarves, Mrs. Ford huddled in an entry way to the Federal Building, leaning against the hot steam radiators. Whenever someone opened the inner door, the blast of warm air buoyed her stench up the wide flight of stairs to the elevator and into the Post Office. My dad joked that her perfumes cleared a head cold. Because everyone in town frequented the Federal Building and the Post Office (there were no mail deliveries then), all were aware that Mrs. Ford also was a volcanic belcher and furious farter. Her gaseous emanations rumbled and counter-pointed her mumblings of "I remember, I remember."

Meanwhile, the town winos fought to stay alive in the grievous cold by hugging those same Federal Building radiators, but not for long. They would get the bum's rush from the U.S. marshals office there. But Mrs. Ford the marshals ushered out kindly, with courtesy. It's one thing to be a bum, without home or hope. It's another to be a rich lady, even a filthy crazy lady with more homes than you could count and with, everyone supposed, stashes of hundred-dollar bills rolled up in quart Mason jars.

When Mrs. Ford came into the N.C. for hardware—she was a constant customer— she always waited for my father to serve her, at least when I was hanging around after school to walk home with my dad. At six-foot-one, truly tall for most men then, Harry de Yonge towered over Mrs. Ford. He treated her with exquisite courtesy, without showing that her aromas had emptied the big hardware department of other customers and compelled other clerks to move to distant storage areas looking for nails to polish. She paid in cash, her half-gloved fingers withdrawing money from a tarnished-silver mesh purse with a top that snapped shut. Her currency, Dad said, was always crisp and new, as if extracted that day from among freshly printed bills the bank kept for its best customers. She ordered with technical precision in a soft, refined voice, down to the merest screw, citing exact size, type, and metal. Few men, Dad said, uttered such precision in dealing with hardware.

For me and other sprats, Mrs. Ford evoked mystery and fear. We talked about her with awe. We keen and inventive liars could recite adventures proving the danger she posed and demonstrating one's own cool head and resourcefulness in the face of an onslaught from the old lady in rags.

If only my bravado about Mrs. Ford echoed some truth. It didn't, and never would. One summer day, Morty Cass and I, both about ten, bicycled past one of Mrs. Ford's derelict houses on lower First Avenue. Upon us descended one of those great thoughts that arrive simultaneously to young male minds deprived of mischief. It came not from our guardian angels. We parked our bikes behind this multi-story log layer-cake, looked around, and pushed against a door. As in Hollywood horror films, it creaked open on rusted hinges. We poked our heads inside, to see a large kitchen, stove, pump, sink, counter, table, chairs, pots and pans on wall hooks, all thick with gray dust and draped in cobwebs interwoven like lace. We nudged inside, sticking close together for courage in the ghastly light filtered through windows that may not have been cleaned in our lifetimes.

"Anybody here?" I shouted. My alto's words sank into silence as heavy as the gloom.

Morty and I slow-marched across the kitchen, kicking up puffs of dust. Morty tried another door. This one didn't groan on its hinges. Ominously, it swung open silently, as if on oiled hinges. It opened into a great living room, two stories high. Like many Fairbanks homes built in the old days, it had a ceiling of caramel-colored, enameled, embossed tin. On a long, rusted chain tethered to the walls by thousands of cobwebs hung the first chandelier I had ever seen, thousands of smudged pieces of diamond-shaped glass. Sticking out of the layer of dust on the floor were pieces of glass that had fallen down. Tall windows, so dirty you couldn't see through them, fronted First Avenue. A large couch fuzzy with dust and more cobwebs sat under the windows. Chairs coated with yet more dust sat randomly around the room. Another window was covered by filthy curtains.

From where we stood, a stairway ran up on our right. Morty and I looked at each other and shrugged. Curiosity stifled fear. We made our way up in a cloud of dust, careful not to touch a banister covered in cobwebs, to a room with a four-poster bed—something else I had never seen except in the movies. Cords tied back the bed's curtains. Under a window sat a piano with its keys exposed.

Suddenly, Morty grunted and grabbed my arm. I heard it, too. Somebody was opening the back door with a screech. We hurtled down the stairs and ran to the front door. It wouldn't open under Morty's desperate tugs. We turned just as a police dog bounded into the room, barking and growling. I peed my pants. Morty screamed. I screamed. A quavering voice said "Sit!" The police dog slid to a halt so close I could smell its breath. All I could see was its fierce eyes and great white fangs and red tongue.

Mrs. Ford, brandishing a big stick, stumped into the room. From her pile of rags her rheumy eyes peered at us. For several eternities, she and the dog and Morty and I froze in tableau. "Back," she said, finally. The dog turned, trotting back to her. "Down," she said. The dog settled to the floor, its eyes blazed on Morty and me menacingly.

"Jackie de Yonge, you get out of here and don't ever let me catch you on my property again. The next time I won't call off the dog. You too, Morty Cass—OUT!"

We edged past her as far away from the dog as possible. Once we hit the kitchen we streaked. We grabbed our bikes on the run and not until we reached the sidewalk did we mount them at high gallop. Winged by pure fear, our Keds thrusting the pedals, Morty raced toward his house on Wendell, I toward mine. My pumping legs squished up and down from where urine soaked my pants and bike seat. There would be only one thing more fearsome than Mrs. Ford—my mother, when she saw that I'd wet my pants. My brain thrashed to invent a lie to satisfy my mom. By the time I neared our cabin, despite years of practice, I still hadn't crafted a lie of sufficient quality to offer my mother. Mrs. Ford might ooze by our house to complain about our trespass, or stop my dad on the street. Any lie I invented now might shrivel later under the heat of truth. Then, Mom would wear out the supply of willows she cut down by the Chena to switch my brother Buzz and me away from waywardness. To Hell with it, I decided. I'd stay away from home and go to earth in the willows, until my pants dried out.

Mrs. Ford never complained to my parents about anything, though she caught me once again, a summer later, with Bobby Burglin, exploring the abandoned store she owned on First Avenue across the street from Fritz's Café. She never got close to us that time, though she saw us. But we saw her first and sprinted to safety out a back door taking refuge in a nearby playground. I never saw Mrs. Ford with the dog again, though I saw her often, summer and winter.

One summer day, the urchins' telegraph relayed that on the other side of town near the smoking, stinking dump, an auction was scheduled to sell a log cabin and its contents.

I bicycled to the cabin and joined the crowd. On a box, towering over us, stood the town's big Englishman, known as the Governor, a hulking cockney with a hooked nose, a toothy smile, and cheeks flushed with the cheer he slugged at intervals from a pint sequestered in a handy pocket. The Governor was the town's chief auctioneer. He also was owner, cook and bottle-washer of the High Spot, a small lunch room across Ninth Avenue from Main School. He catered to school kids, dishing out hot dogs, hamburgers, toasted cheese sandwiches, milk shakes, soda pop, and pie à la mode.

From his box the Governor delivered his spiel. Behind him crouched the cabin, with an open door, and spread out on the ground nearby were chairs, piles of clothes, tables, dishes, curtains, shovels, and rakes. He had hired a kid as an assistant to fetch an item at his command and hold it up, while the Governor extolled its virtues and tickled the onlookers with come-ons to get them bidding. I'd hung out at a number of these outdoor auctions, always in the summer for obvious reasons, which were staged to pay off some poor bankrupt occupant's debts. We practiced gawkers knew the big deal would be the house and lot. Selling the rest of the stuff, mainly junk, was only a warm-up.

A Pioneer Cab pulled up, and Mrs. Ford emerged. The crowd murmured. None of us ever had seen her in a cab before. Someone wondered aloud how any driver could stand being in a car with her stench. The answer, of course, was money. Mrs. Ford tendered the driver a twenty—the going price for a whore, I had learned delivering newspapers—and waved off the change.

The old woman was like Moses. The crowd parted as she toddled up to the Governor, who beamed down on her from his box with a broad smile.

"Just in time, just in time, dear lady," he said, "I knew you were coming and I've saved the best for the last so that you could bless us with your presence before we put this excellent domicile and demesne up for bidding."

Mrs. Ford was not the only one in the crowd intent on buying the cabin and lot. In the back, a man in a sports jacket and slacks topped Mrs. Ford bid for bid. The Governor asked for one thousand dollars. Onlookers murmured. Mrs. Ford nodded, now standing by herself, with everyone else at least ten feet away, downwind. The stranger flicked a finger.

"I have 1,050 dollars," the Governor droned. "Who'll make that even 1,100. Dear Lady?"

Mrs. Ford nodded. The bidding continued for nearly ten more minutes. With a final nod, Mrs. Ford offered a bid that forced a silence from the gent in the rear, who turned and walked away.

"Done! Sold!" shouted the Governor, throwing out his arms, then bending down to offer his hand to Mrs. Ford. He glowed, thinking of his commission.

The Governor always insisted on payment in cash or by certified check. If the check was made out for more than the successful bid, he would make change for it in cash. If the check was less, the bidder had to hand over the difference in cash. Like all Fairbanks business people, the Governor had been burned accepting personal checks. The joke went that if you could make tires from all the checks that bounced in Fairbanks, you could solve the wartime rubber shortage. We all pressed forward to watch Mrs. Ford finish the transaction.

"Do you want to wait?" the Governor asked as he jumped down from his box. He brought forth a gray metal lock-box and .45 Colt automatic and asked us all to step back ten paces—"Thank you very much, dear friends, you understand the necessity of a modicum of privacy while I and the dear lady finish our business."

While he was doing this, Mrs. Ford's hands burrowed into the dry goods mounding her body. Her hands ran around like two small dogs under a blanket. A hand reappeared holding a Mason jar. We gasped. It was one of the rumored jars!

The jar was green with money. Ignoring the curious crowd, Mrs. Ford unscrewed the top, with blackened fingers fished out a roll of hundred-dollar bills, and counted them out into a pile. The Governor barely glanced at the money while resting his right hand on the pistol and surveying the crowd. When she stopped, he thanked her, swept the bills into his box, and locked it. He pulled papers out of his jacket, wrote on them, signed them, handed them to Mrs. Ford. She shoved them into her garments along with the Mason jar.

"That's all, that's all," the Governor called. "Good-bye, good-bye, dear friends, we'll expect you the next time. Good-bye."

With lock box and .45 in hand he climbed quickly into a nearby blue Ford coupe. He shoved on the starter, put the coupe in gear, waved, and drove off with a puff of exhaust. Then the Pioneer Cab returned. The driver hopped out, opening the rear door for Mrs. Ford with a smile. She pushed in. End of spectacle.

When Dad came home to dinner that night, he told my mom while mixing a Tom Collins that somebody had clubbed Mrs. Ford over the head and robbed her. Someone found her unconscious, bleeding around the face, in the alley next to the Piggly Wiggly market. She had been taken to the hospital.

"Imagine how the sisters and nurses must have held their noses to undress her," Mom shuddered.

"They'll hose her down with steam once they've bandaged her head," Dad said. We all laughed.

Years later, fresh out of college and proud to have become a reporter at the *News-Miner*, I'd often see Mrs. Ford as I worked my beats at the police station, City Hall, the courts, and the marshal's office at the Federal Building. So far as I could tell, she had not changed the clothes I remembered from boyhood. I always said hello. Her eyes now looked like Orphan Annie's, blank and white with cataracts. When I was a boy, I thought of her as large. Now I found she did not come up to my armpit. Probably she was shrinking with age inside her fortress of garments.

One day at lunch, I talked about her with the town's leading physician and my doctor and a territorial senator, Doctor Paul Haggland, a Republican of infinite medical and political skills. "Each time she comes into the hospital," he said, "we use a standard routine. With a small electric saw that I use in bone surgeries, we saw her clothes off. We have to. Her body fluids have so saturated the dozen layers she wears that they have fused together, like a shell. Think of her as a turtle, a tiny old lady turtle, in a big shell, whose body we have to expose in order to find out what's wrong with her and treat her.

"We wear gloves and masks to do this," he said, "because she is so filthy. Even though I've autopsied many drowned bloats, I've got to admit her smell would gag a statue. And she always has lice. We put a mild chemical on our masks that blanks out her smell. Once we fix her up—usually these days she's fainted from being dehydrated and undernourished—we shave all but her head hair to clear the lice. We wash her, every orifice and crevice. The nurses rinse her head with louse killer; comb out the lice, nits, and eggs; wash her hair, dry it, trim it, and put it up in a bow. Then we put a fresh gown on her. We cut her fingernails and toenails. We brush her gums and rinse them. She has no teeth anymore. Then we feed her. She never talks to us, but once she's been bathed and tidied, she will smile. I'll come in with cups of tea to drink with her and talk to her. Her tea I lace with a sleep draught. Aside from not eating well, people like her, if only because of the lice, have a hard time sleeping and are constantly tired. When she's ready to go home, we dress her in decent clothes the sisters have rustled up. I talk to her about changing her ways. I give her drugs and prescriptions for refills. Finally she goes off in a cab.

"In a couple of days, I'll see her on the street. In what appears to be the same dirty pile of rags we cut off of her. I'll say hello. She'll just slide on by without acknowledgment.

"One of my more successful cases," he laughed. I bought us another round of martinis before we lunched.

Here is what the *News-Miner* said about her a few months later, on February 22, 1957 (I was still working for the paper, and may have written these unsigned words):

"At 3:55 p.m. yesterday, death ended the strange and tragic career of Mrs. Hulda Ford, the ragged little lady who prowled the town's streets and alleys.

"She died at St. Joseph's Hospital at the age of 83. The lady who picked through downtown trash cans when she thought nobody was looking owned property at the time of her death worth approximately $500,000, and has thousands more in cash deposited in local banks.

"The full extent of her fortune will probably not be known for a long time. Her estate consists of valuable rental property, vacant lots, old buildings, and cash. But the city and the Internal Revenue Service have claims against her holdings due to delinquent taxes."

Rest in peace, Hulda.

Eighteen

BRAWLS AND FISTFIGHTS

During my boyhood all of Fairbanks was divided into three parts: Homeland (sanctuary), No Boys Land (perilous) and Other Boys Land (dangerous).

Homeland was Wendell Avenue and an area roughly a half-mile south and a half-mile west, toward town. Two families of boys there ruled over me. The Hemans lived directly across the street and the Burnettes lived down the street a block. As a little boy, I learned that if I intruded where the twins George and Gerard Heman were playing, it had to be with their permission, sometimes granted with a nod or sign, sometimes denied with a wave, especially as they grew older, learning about and practicing sex and extending their immediate fiefdom to the thick willows along the Chena behind their house. Four years older than I, the twins enforced the law that applies all across the animal world: bigger and older dominates smaller and younger.

If I insisted on intruding without visa, one or the other Heman with a swift fist would arch the distance from his shoulder to my nose. Bawling, mucous and blood bubbling from my snout, I'd run home, yowling, whereupon my mother would screech out into the street or down into the willows to render justice unto George and Gerard. A little experience with her as harpy diving upon them, talons ready to clutch and render, taught them to flee home. There, upon their bursting into her kitchen, Mrs. Heman, a spare, older woman about half my mom's size, would scamper out to chitter a barrage of ire that my mom returned in kind, with interest. In the summer, these wars of words would attract neighbors out into the street, eager for entertainment.

More than Wendell Avenue divided mother de Yonge and her two sons from the Hemans. The Hemans also practiced Catholicism, but of a German brand my mother thought suspicious because she identified Germans with Luther. The Heman clan, of which there were many, trooped off to a different Sunday mass than we. When the war started, anti-German prejudice immediately clacked neighborhood tongues against the Hemans, as it did against every other family in town with a German name, including the parents of my best school friend, Alfred Baumeister. Two elder Heman brothers went off to war, as I recollect. That muted patriotic gossip. One brother, Denny, returned home badly wounded, ripped by flak over Germany.

I courted the twins. Although they treated me as a serf, the Hemans would protect me from run-ins with any of the Burnettes, who lived in a house made of lumber that stood out among the log cabins. The Burnettes were numerous. The Burnette boys, the Hemans, and I inherited a primitive world where male territorialism reined supreme. You controlled the space around you, by fighting if necessary, or you bowed to those who did. That meant they could shove you around, shake you down for money and smokes and sometimes sex, and otherwise make life miserable. If Burnette males ventured onto our block, the Hemans would attack. Sometimes a Burnette and a Heman would square off for a most entertaining and fulfilling fight with blood, sweat, snot, and sometimes teeth flying. As a matter of honor, we picked up stray teeth to return to their owner.

To the south and west, other boys asserted dominance, but they were not so much trouble for me. This was because in school, all of us who lived near each other vaguely thought of ourselves as allies against the rest of the meaningful universe, i.e., boys from other parts of town.

Boys' fighting was so common that not until I went away to college did I come to understand that some young males actually grew up without having swung fists, kicked balls, or gouged eyes.

Once I left the immediate environs of Wendell Avenue, I entered No Boys Land. This encompassed the downtown business core of Fairbanks and the area a couple of blocks on either side of Cushman Street, then the main north-south thoroughfare. Here, I was wise to travel with friends—Al Baumeister, Bob Burglin, Morty Cass, Seward Olsen, and especially the Heman twins if they would let me, in order not to get ambushed by other boys who, while they might not have disliked me, if they were more numerous or bigger and stronger, would go after me like dogs go after a cat. This was nothing personal, just great sport.

In this area I knew not only every alley way, byway, and short-cut but also what stores, such as Lavery's dry good store or Adler's Bookstore, both on Cushman Street, might offer sanctuary. The Adlers were Jewish and appreciated one fleeing from many. They also knew me as a constant browser and sometimes buyer of books. Therefore, they welcomed a waif into the best place in town for not being bored while waiting for enemies outside the door to abandon their vigil and disappear.

My best bastion was the N.C., the biggest commercial establishment in Fairbanks, on First Avenue a block west of Cushman Street. The N.C. machine shop, telephone building, and warehouses occupied the block behind the store. If, on the run, I reached these asylums, where I was known as Harry de Yonge's boy, I was safe.

Other Boys Land was everywhere else in Fairbanks and out of town. From adventures, friendships, and alliances usually made in school but shifting constantly, I knew where other boys lived and, depending on time of year, weather and other variables, controlled and patrolled various pieces of Fairbanks turf. The Iceberg boys dominated a block or two just east of Main School but generally were benign toward me. The Straights, a particularly aggressive set of brothers over on Seventh Avenue beyond Barnette Street, would chase me down and pummel me just for the exercise. Across the Chena from my place and easily accessible in the winter, when cars crossed the river on the ice, was Graehl, home of the O'Leary family, a tribe that I regarded as savages.

In the summer, I rarely saw an O'Leary, and then chiefly downtown, where I could escape easily or where I had friends who would back me if, after a trade of insults, one of the O'Learys and I would engage in a fistfight that amused barflies and passersby. But in the winter, the damned O'Learys crossed the river ice to parade by my house displaying, if they saw me, ungloved middle fingers in the air. They never seemed to scrape the Hemans' sensibilities, however.

In late winter, when thaws came and went, my friends and I built elaborate snow forts with walls sometimes six feet high, embattlements whose sloping outer walls we iced with buckets of water dragged from home. These fortifications could be entered only through a slit door. Once frozen, the outside walls were too slick to be climbable without a ladder and too thick to breach while defenders inside, standing on raised platforms of pounded snow, rained iced snowballs down on invaders. Several times, following diagrams traced from encyclopedias, we built inner walls in a maze for easy defense.

On a warm Saturday one March, a half-dozen O'Learys and their allies attacked me, my brother, Mort Cass, and a couple of other boys while we sat in our ice fort smoking cigarettes and eating army rations filched from Army trucks parked a few blocks away on Lacey Street. A battle of bloody noses, black eyes, bruises, cuts, and other wounds followed. Our magazine was full of iced snowballs, and we battled the invaders for hours until finally some parents figured out what was going on and dispersed us all. Buzz and I caught hell at home because of our injuries and because we were fighting with other good Catholics. I did not bother to explain to Mom that many of the people I disliked, feared, and even hated were Catholics. I refused to ration out my antipathies to Protestants only. There were enough for all.

Alfred Baumeister, one of the best athletes and students of my generation of frontier-town youngsters, later to become a major academic, author, and national expert on retardation, was wiry and quick—a wildcat among us. Because he also was short and light, a temptation existed among us to try to bully him with size and weight. He also had a name that caused the less cautious to slur him between 1941 and 1945 as a dirty German responsible for all of Adolph Hitler's evils, an honor he refused to accept. (His mother and stepfather left Germany to get away from Hitler.) Alfred also had a wit that could sting almost as quickly as his well-respected right jab.

I hadn't known Alfred long in kindergarten before we got into a sandbox fight. That day, I learned a lifelong lesson: even if you were bigger, it did not pay to fight with one who never gave up, who hit, kicked, bit, gouged if necessary, even if ultimately your weight wore him down. The cost of victory was too much. Over some years, for reasons I cannot remember, I tested Alfred's defensive skills several times and found them each time just as painfully effective as the time before. I watched others take Alfred on and regret it, too, even if it could be said the aggressor won the fight. I had not heard of King Pyrrhus until I reached college, but when I did, thanks to having tangled with Baumeister, I understood the devastating cost of a Pyrrhic victory.

Baumeister and I and others followed the loose leadership of Bob Burglin, whose mother operated an office-supply store on Cushman Street. Burglin was a bright, gawky kid who for no apparent reason was the best fighter among us. He never ducked battle and seemed to like fighting, something I cannot say for myself. He also was witty and had something the rest of us rarely had—abundant spending money, from his mother's purse and from his own many little side businesses with other urchins.

He dominated kids his age on the playgrounds and at important principalities such as the ballparks and, in the spring, the marble-shooting grounds at the school and on the south side of the Federal Building. When the dirt reappeared in the spring, our pockets bulged and clicked with marbles. Commerce in marbles, with rules more arcane than those that govern the Chicago Board of Trade, distracted us in school, infuriated teachers, and caused the marble-shooting fields to host as many wars as Flanders. The marble games we played required not just skills in shooting, lagging, positioning, and reckoning. Intellectual depth was necessary as well to comprehend a vast array of rules and regulations.

Burglin excelled at marbles, at the marble trade, at marble lawyering and perhaps most important, in securing a patch of dirt on the sun side of the Federal Building on which to play. Fights often erupted not only in competition for space, the rampant cheating that took place as we knuckled down with our shooters, and the mercilessly taking in combat of another player's supply of glassies, pasties, or, God willing, agates, but also over the demolishing of a boy's hopes, his spirits, his very soul. Burglin faced constant challenges, never backed off, and usually won.

The best fist-fight during my boyhood matched Burglin against Ron Dodson of a famous Fairbanks flying family and later an airline pilot himself. I cannot remember the cause. In school one day the word passed: Burglin and Dodson would go at it in the truck-loading dock behind the Federal Building. Immediately, we began calculating the betting odds. Dodson, a good guy, knew how to use his fists, feet, and teeth. He had a husky build to lend authority to his punches and kicks. We all had become sophisticated bettors having observed gambling in the Fairbanks bars and hotels and from betting on boxing matches broadcast on radio. I had made money off Joe Louis, my hero. One didn't bet merely on who would win but by how much and for how long, with what injuries, and so forth.

On this spring afternoon, after four o'clock when the federal employees had gone home, about one hundred boys and men gathered at the loading dock. Silver dollars and five-dollar bills flashed and bets were marked down. Cliques arranged themselves for cheering and jeering. A man took it upon himself to referee, not rounds—there were no such niceties in our fights—but for fair fighting. We deemed out of bounds all hair-pulling, eye-gouging, testicle-squeezing, ear-biting, and rabbit punches, unless you could get away with them. We had ethics, after all. We were Americans.

At the drop of a handkerchief, Burglin and Dodson came out punching. Bare fists pummeled eyes and mouths. Blood flew from split lips. Sweat spattered. Grunts sounded. Cheers, howls, and catcalls echoed. These two boys, eleven or twelve, gave no quarter, nor wanted any. They grappled. They fell. They wrestled. One would break free, rise, and kick the other's ribs until once again they faced each other with swelling faces, knuckles plunging into flushed or blackening flesh. After what seemed like a long time, both staggered, exhausted, shuffling forward to punch weakly again, before having to drop arms just to rest, staring at each other, spitting blood. Shouted odds and bets rang off the concrete walls. Amazingly, neither gladiator had lost a tooth.

At last, they could fight no longer—a draw, a goddamned draw. This was a disappointment to all of us who had made bets. But it was a hell of a fight, well worth the free admission.

Nineteen

PEDDLING NEWSPAPERS

In June, 1942, the same month my mother sold my services to pick cutworms in Mr. Jacobs' cabbage patch, the Japanese bombed Dutch Harbor in the Aleutian Islands and invaded Kiska and Attu in a futile attempt to lure the American fleet away from Midway Island in the Pacific.

Dad got out his rifles again and reported that sales of ammo were brisk at the N.C. hardware.

No matter that the attackers were farther from Fairbanks than Denver is from Washington, D.C., with a wilderness in between. All the adults worried that those slant-eyed bastards soon would charge up Cushman Street with bayonets fixed, screaming "Banzai!"

Worried, too, for a while, were the politicians, editorial-writers, and military, not that Fairbanks had much military presence other than the ACS boys who took care of the telegraph lines and several score of personnel at Ladd Field, the Army's new cold-weather testing post southeast of town, which had two airstrips so that the Army Air Corps could find out how fighters and bombers fared in fifty below zero.

By the end of that summer, Fairbanks was experiencing its second great boom. The gold rush upon which Fairbanks was founded in 1902 attracted ten-thousand lusting prospectors and miners, but most soon drifted away empty-handed. By 1939, the Fairbanks-area population had withered to about two-thousand souls, many living on beans and bacon so that they could save for a ticket on a southbound train. Then, the tide turned, as upwards of ten-thousand thirsty, lusty, and lonely soldiers and airmen, not to mention many more construction workers, flooded stores, saloons, restaurants, churches, and the red-light district. Ladd Field bustled with airplane traffic and contractors, told not to worry about cost, hastily erected barracks, officers' quarters, theaters, mess halls, a command headquarters, hangars, and repair shops—everything needed to keep the Air Corps flying. Work began on an emergency airfield at 26 Mile on the Richardson Highway, later to become one of the nation's largest air bases, Eielson Air Force Base. New arrivals also included members of the Women's Army Corps, Red Cross workers, and civilian workers, and carpetbaggers.

In the fall, a rumor circulated around town that a bunch of Russian officers had flown into Ladd Field and that more were coming. This was a top-secret arrival.

The rumor was true. It was part of the U.S.-Soviet Lend-Lease Program to help the Russians fight the Germans in Europe. Within the year, hundreds of Russian pilots, mechanics, and support crews arrived wearing tight belted uniforms, high boots, and Stalin hats, along with officers wearing small pistols holstered on their hips, medals jangling. The pilots were doomed men, as it turned out. No one suspected then that if they didn't die ferrying American planes across the Arctic wastes and

Bering Straits to Siberia and eventually to Russia's western front, assuming they survived the war, that Stalin's secret police would order most of them shot for having been tainted with dangerous American capitalistic ideas imported from Fairbanks, Alaska.

Fairbanks thrived on vice, one of its gold-rush mainstays. Within months, every other establishment along First and Second avenues had metamorphosed into a dark cigarette-littered bar, juke box blaring, crowded at all hours, jammed on weekends. Especially wild were monthly paydays and holidays when parched and lonely carpenters, pipefitters, electricians, bulldozer operators and other construction workers came to town with money in their pockets, mixing with white American GIs, few older than twenty and far from home. (The Army refused to allow black soldiers off post, keeping them segregated there and housing them in tents even during the coldest weather.)

Russian pilots and other Russian officers joined our lusty and parched proletarians and warriors in the Fairbanks saloons and whorehouses, proving to be the thirstiest of them all. I watched the Russians slug down free snorts from Americans while our government, newspapers, magazines and movies characterized Joe Stalin as one of the saviors of civilization.

No Nose Nelly, Dynamite Red, and a dozen other prostitutes in the officially unofficial Fourth Avenue red-light district labored patriotically to satisfy the spermous needs of the horny military youths and construction workers who poured into town.

A line of men, with tent poles in their pants, as my mother remarked, not thinking I would understand, snaked along Turner Street waiting to enter the back alley of the cribs of the Whore Line. The boom attracted new hustlers to town, ready for business. Without permits from City Hall, the newcomers marketed their sexual services in the bars. Such interlopers stirred rumbles of distress from established prostitutes and from town fathers who owned property on Fourth Avenue. The chief excuse for tolerating a formal red-light district there, even if it was only a block long and on one side of the street, sprang from the theory that centralized sex-for-pay sponged up the dangerous lechery of all males from sixteen to 106. The monthly permits the town fathers sold to the Fourth Avenue sporting ladies required them to get monthly medical examinations. Such look-sees, according to the prevailing view, protected whores' customers against what polite babble of the day called "social diseases"—forms of nastiness that my mother, my teachers and my priests warned me against contracting.

These warnings puzzled me. Who wanted to catch a bad disease deliberately?

No one explained to us what these diseases were and they only hinted about how they were acquired. By the time I was nine, however, the common intelligence shared by boys in school assured me that one caught a social disease—the clap, blue balls, and the weeping dick—by engaging in the fascinating activity of sticking your peter into certain women. Penetrating men, or being penetrated by them, never was mentioned in this regard. At any rate, I reckoned that I was in small danger of contracting a social disease.

Worse from the standpoint of public morals was that, unlike the well-established Fourth Avenue women, the freelancers paid not a penny to the leaders of the established order. Untaxed exchanges of body fluids took place along the public thoroughfares with female, homosexual, and transsexual prostitutes working out of the backseats of cars (in the summer, chiefly, but not always) and in the backrooms of bars.

How did I as a mere child learn all this? Adults gossiped often about the Whore Line, its denizens, and its rumored and its actual proprietors.

I also had a ticket allowing me to view the sporting scene, the whorehouse cribs, the bars, and gambling joints: I sold newspapers. I sold newspapers every afternoon for years to the ladies of Whore Line. Once I turned eight, Mom had decided it was time for me to earn my keep, or part of it. Selling papers offered steadier work than picking worms off cabbages. At her direction, I presented myself downtown at *Jessen's Weekly* and became a paper boy. She advanced me three silver dollars. With other waifs entering into the free enterprise of peddling the press, I duly handed these to Mr. Jessen, a jolly, gray-haired, round-faced man who wore Ben Franklin spectacles, at the front counter of his print shop. There, I first smelled a perfume that beguiled me the rest of my life: fresh ink on warm newsprint.

The place rumbled, rattled, and roared from the presses flapping and rolling in the rear. Mr. Jessen took my three dollars, thanked me, counted and handed me twenty newly printed copies of his weekly. He sold me, on credit, a stained canvas newspaper bag with a shoulder strap. "You owe me a dollar for that. Don't forget, Jackie," he said. "Say hello to your mom and dad for me. Next."

I was to sell each copy for twenty-five cents, yielding a profit of two dollars, not a bad return. At Mom's suggestion, I knocked on doors along Wendell Avenue and offered to deliver the paper every week. Soon I had created a *Jessen's Weekly* paper route that my brother and I serviced for the next six years.

Selling the weekly produced profits, but Alfred Baumeister and Bob Burglin told me the real money was made selling the *Daily News-Miner*, too, on the streets and especially in the bars and whorehouses. Tips usually exceeded the nickels earned from a sale—a whole dollar sometimes, now and then a fiver, with the fattest tips coming from the Russians when their snoots glowed with booze and homesickness. When the final school bell rang, even on cold days, my pals and I rushed downtown to buy copies of the *News-Miner* to hawk on the streets. The first guys out shouting headlines sold the most papers the fastest. Even better, my friends reported, no reason existed in the universe to tell anyone, especially your parents, about your tips. They were your jingle, to spend as you wanted. Naturally, discretion ruled. It was not wise to bring home things that called attention to your spending power and resulted in shakedowns and taxing demands. No sane boy wanted either.

I joined the mob of boys who raced to a *News-Miner* loading dock on First Avenue to pick up the first copies to slap off the rotary press that vibrated in the paper's cavernous pressroom in the Chena Building, adjacent to the Lathrop Building, where the rest of the newspaper staff worked. The loading dock had a drop door that warded off rain, wind and snow but not summer's dust and mud or winter's cold. It provided a Spartan-like haven of cold concrete, the roar of the press, the boys' shouting, and dim overhead lights.

Some days, while waiting for the press to roll, we battled boredom by lagging pennies, nickels, dimes, quarters, four-bit pieces, even silver dollars against a wall. The contestant whose coin slid closest to the wall won all the money. Here I learned to play blackjack and poker, always for money, and learned about being cheated at cards and how to cheat. Fights erupted, especially over cheating. The paper's circulation bosses didn't like a fracas. They'd wade into fights, grab pugilists by the coats or shirts or ears and jerk them apart, issuing dire warnings that they would kick out the next boy who threw a punch. Here, too, I cemented alliances, especially with Al Baumeister. He backed me. I backed him.

The newspapers, whether the daily or the weekly and later even the daily *Seattle Star*, imported by air each day to sell for $1 a copy to the swelling hordes of military and construction workers, gave me and other newsboys access to bars, the Whore Line, the hospital, sundry mercantile establishments and offices, even to Ladd Field, where ordinary mortals had to produce passes at the gates. The Military Police guards would glance at us and our newspapers and wave us through. Wise newsboys left free copies for the guards. Quid and Pro Quo early became our business partners.

I loved the saloons, especially in the winter. Men and women jammed them day and night in a murky haze of cigarette, pipe, and cigar smoke. Music blared from juke boxes and from one of my favorite machines that I love to this day—a device as big as a standup Coke machine, but with a big glass screen. Slip it a silver dollar and a short movie reel of a jazz orchestra would play and singers sing. By hanging around the Silver Dollar Bar or the Chena Bar or the Arctic Bar, among many others, waiting for some adult denizen to plunk in a buck, I came to hear and appreciate Louis Armstrong, Duke Ellington, Count Basie, Bennie Goodman, Gene Krupa. The list is long and illustrious. Listening to this music in those frontier saloons implanted in me an everlasting taste.

The bars produced big tips. Often I'd get a silver dollar for a two-bit newspaper, with a slurred, "Keep the change, kid." I'd pipe lavish thanks and hustle to the next potential customer. I learned not to bother men and women wrapped in each other's body. They wanted what I could not provide—privacy, pleasure, and orgasms. I learned to dodge the hands of men who reached for my crotch or butt. In those days, the culture deemed goosing a kid an innocent sport. As for screwing a kid, if it wasn't rape, the law didn't worry about it, though it did worry that the kid's old man might exact revenge with fists, bat, knife, or gun. That would disturb the public peace. Town cops and military cops valued the public peace more than justice.

I computed how much money to give my mother and how much to hide from her. Such calculation required intense thought. Mom anticipated that I would get tips. She wanted those, too. I learned that if she discovered comic books or candy or other treats on me that cost more money than she gave me in a weekly allowance—a pittance by my standards—her demands for explanation could lure me into perilous lies that, if discovered, resulted in some serious switching on her part. Consequently, I blew what I reckoned to be my share of tips playing pinball and slot machines. Both festooned Fairbanks, and not just in saloons, but also in Greimann's Bus Depot, in barber shops, sandwich joints, and in the clubs—the Shriners, Eagles, and Elks.

For high scores, the pinballs paid off in coin at the cash register, sometimes large amounts to a skilled player or to an accomplished cheat who had drilled the machine to insert a wire to trip the score up (and, to avoid suspicion, only milked the machine now and then).

As for the slots, we boys discussed such erudite matters as timing: being ready to jump in front of a slot and deposit a nickel, dime, quarter, fifty-cent piece or silver dollar the moment a losing player moved away to scratch, pee, buy more coins, or light a smoke. Because slot owners set the machines to cough back a pittance of the coins they consumed, to keep the suckers playing, we theorized that jumping in at the right time gave us a break on the odds. It didn't, of course, but occasionally one of us hit a payout, the news of which re-enforced our flawed thinking.

Great fights erupted in the bars. Sometimes the combatants swarmed into the street, even during the coldest temperatures. Word flashed around the downtown gin mills. We paper boys rushed to the event. Bar battles included not just bare knuckles but also broken bottles. Town cops and MPs, American and Russian, responded swiftly. Town police tended to be big-bellied men too old for military service. There weren't many of them. They often appeared one or two at a time, unhappy because they'd been enjoying a free beer and a smoke in the back of another bar. They tended to be talkers and placators, swinging their billy clubs only when desperate. They often picked the least-pugnacious gladiators to arrest as examples of what could happen to the others.

The Military Police were fit, lean, and mean. They traveled in fours, two American MPs and two Russian MPs. They could not arrest civilians. But they collared the military with gusto, wading into a crowd with clubs flailing. The Americans slammed the American GIs across the back or behind the ear while leaving the officers alone. The Russians beat any Russian in the fray, even officers, with savage whomps to the face and forehead. The MPs dragged the cold-cocked or crippled to a canvas-covered truck idling on the street and threw their prey inside.

The Ladd Field honor guard that raised and lowered Old Glory every day outside of post headquarters marched with precision and skill. The honor guard had lots of practice. It was made up of prisoners from the post brig, forced to parade and look spiffy. I heard that the Russians hauled in by their MPs were not so fortunate. Those prisoners were flown back to Russia to serve on the front lines, where chances of survival were near zero.

Selling newspapers on the Whore Line was a right I earned and sustained with my fists. Other newsboys wanted access to this market. Any challenge had to be settled fist-to-nose because the ladies working in the Fourth Avenue cribs were choice customers. They usually were home and not too busy in mid-afternoon. They wanted a paper to read between tricks. They were nice to me, and later to my brother when he helped me sell papers. They knew us. They liked to chat. They were so generous that I came to take their tips for granted in calculating what the day's income would be.

Working the Whore Line provided me an early education in the vagaries of lust. Most afternoons only a few customers strolled the alley where many cabins offered display windows behind which a lady displayed herself. On quiet days, I inspected the merchandise at leisure, unless the working girl indicated with hand signals that I should move on. All the women were white. The town's authorities enforced racial discrimination in whoredom with vigor. Upon demand from prospective customers, younger prostitutes—some were still adolescent—would elevate a light robe to flash themselves naked from the neck down and "fan their annies," as it was called. Thus, I learned the general map of female anatomy. Others wore elaborate costumes including black mesh stockings, stiletto high heels, and black leather gloves that reached to their armpits. Still others simply sat in chairs, often with a newspaper or a Bible, in ordinary street clothes, smiling, looking like somebody's mom inviting you in for cookies and milk.

On paydays, would-be partakers of the flesh queued for blocks at the entrance to the Line, even on winter days. If the weather was half tolerable, those in line would buy papers to read during the slow shuffle forward. They weren't good tippers, though.

To the day she died, my mother refused to admit that my little brother and I hawked newspapers on the Whore Line. Her standards, nay, the vaunted moral standards of World War II Fairbanks itself, would not allow for children to consort with prostitutes, touching money filthy from their hands and the hands of their depraved customers. I liked to set my mother fuming by remarking about the big red and yellow boxes of chocolates I sometimes dragged home, fancy boxes two or three layers deep, with satin bows on the outside. These were given to me by prostitutes who had more candy than they could eat, given to them by customers with access to the Ladd Field Post Exchange, a fairyland stuffed with goods the war had stripped from civilian shelves. I'd ask Mom: where do you think I got the chocolates at a time when civilians could not buy such luxuries because of wartime shortages? Despite her fuming, Mom dearly loved chocolates and at the time seemed most happy to take them from my innocent hands.

Later I expanded my newspaper commerce to Ladd Field, working the huge mess halls thrown up all over the post by the construction contractors laying down runways, erecting concrete and metal hangars, building housing and barracks and administrative offices, and those military facilities upon which the nation's security and survival depend—the enlisted men's club, noncoms' club and most important of all, the officers' club, all with thriving bars. Underground tunnels linked the main facilities so that one could walk to and fro without ever getting above ground, a great boon on frigid days.

The military ran shuttle buses between the post and downtown Fairbanks. I could hop a bus downtown with an armload of papers and ride for free. The *Seattle Star* was the best-selling newspaper to this clientele. I often headed for a long, noisy mess hall operated by a contractor. It seated hundreds of dust-stained men in work clothes eating immense servings of steaks, chops, cutlets and potatoes, boiled onions, peas, green beans, mixed salads, pies, cakes, cupcakes, ice cream, all carried to the tables on large brown trays by women in white and black waitress outfits. I got good tips there, too. Many of the men liked to talk about baseball or school or fishing. I could eat with them if I wanted—no charge. No one ever said a thing except sit down and we'll serve you some grub.

Ladd Field maintained a stock of Army Air Corps fighter planes and bombers for cold-weather testing and defense until the Japanese were turned back in the Pacific. By then, scores of planes being transferred to Russia had started to arrive after a long series of hops from the Lower 48 up through Alberta and British Columbia, from air strip to air strip in remote hamlets along the newly bulldozed Alaska Highway. American pilots piloted these planes, grousing at a duty that kept them from combat in Europe or the Pacific. Ferrying fighters and bombers won no one any glory.

I loved going near the fighters and bombers lined up awaiting the Russians to fly them to the west. New Russian pilots arriving in transport aircraft from Siberia and Kamchatka flew the planes to learn the controls and avionics. We loved to watch their aerobatics high above us, sketched by long, white contrails of ice crystals. The occasional crashes thrilled us. Once, as we set out on bicycles for Ladd Field, we saw a big, black oily cloud suddenly appear. This time, security at the gate stopped us, to our morbid disappointment.

Planes included the Lockheed P-38 Lightening, a twin-boomed, ground-attack fighter; Bell P-39 Airacobras (fighters); North American B-25 Mitchell and Douglas A-20 light bombers; and Curtis-Wright C-46 and Douglas C-47 transports. We boys examined and memorized them all. They roared into the skies around Fairbanks by the hundreds every month by late 1942, first to Ladd Field and later to the new airfield being hastily built and expanded at 26 Mile. When word came that Uncle Sam would pour hundreds of millions of dollars into new air strips out on the moose flats south of town, my folks and neighbors and the N.C. friends who dropped by after work for a quick snort and a little gossip at our kitchen table all talked about the new base becoming a launching point for air strikes against Japan.

The Army air generals knew better. The excuse for the base was that it was needed as an alternative landing area for the planes headed for Russia. In fact, the deeper thinkers in the Pentagon believed the United States would need a base from which it could launch attack bombers to impress Joe Stalin and his fellow Communists in the Kremlin. It would be quicker and easier to fly a U.S. bomber from 26 Mile to Red Square than from virtually any other habitable site in North America. These were the days before the nuclear bomb existed, but some high ranking officials knew that work on it was underway and that if it worked, a powerful new bomb would intimidate the world. They did not know that spies working on the project or working for British Intelligence would deliver the bomb's science, technology and blueprints to the Kremlin.

From the beginning of the wartime Lend-Lease program that handed over the P-38s, P-39s, B-25s and other war planes to waiting Russian crews at Fairbanks, our military kept the

Russians away from 26 Mile. Looking back, I cannot but think the Russians boozing in Fairbanks bars, visiting civilian homes, and attending civilian parties and dances had to have heard of the great military base being built. Everybody talked about 26 Mile and what was going on out there. It wasn't much of a secret in Fairbanks.

Local citizens hailed the Russians as true heroes. My dad helped arrange dinner parties and picnics for the visiting allies, most of them young men. I'm not quite sure how he got involved. For a couple of years, we had Russian airmen and officers as frequent guests at our dinner table, at holiday parties, and on outings to Harding Lake. I once had a collection of medals and gilded buttons that the visiting Russians plucked from their uniforms to give to a boy and his little brother. My dad befriended a White Russian, an engineer who had been on the wrong side in the Russian Civil War of 1918-21, when the Red Army forced the last anti-Soviet troops out of the Crimea. This friend, whose name escapes my memory and who could not be found in the records, dined frequently with us and acted as interpreter for the Russian officers and enlisted men who also were guests in our home.

One afternoon, rather than trudge home in the biting, bitter winter darkness after peddling papers, I went to the N.C. hardware to walk home with my dad.

Just at closing time, the White Russian showed up with a uniformed Russian officer—an older man, short, bow-legged in his high boots, wearing a great unbuttoned, fur-collared overcoat that hung to the floor. Both were, as my father used to say, high as a kite, in rollicking high spirits, and they hunted for dad. He and I were just bundling up for the twenty-minute trek home through the ice fog. They wanted wine, lots of it, for a party. It may sound strange to those who knew Fairbanks then, or Fairbanks now, that they simply didn't buy some at one of the scores of liquor stores. But in 1943, bottles of varietal wines of the kinds now common on American tables did not exist in Fairbanks.

The chief wine of the day was sweet goo from New York bottled under the label Virginia Dare. The N.C., however, did have in huge casks a red dry wine that it sold by the gallon, bring your own container. The White Russian knew of this, but alas had arrived with his new Soviet friend just as the store closed. No wine to be had. They appealed to my father for help.

To honor the great alliance between Russians and Americans to whip the Germans, my dad took up the challenge. With the Russians and me in tow, he went forth to find Ed Clausen, one of his oldest and dearest hunting and fishing companions and by then a major boss in the N.C. establishment. Ed immediately saw that the war effort required his cooperation. Keys in hand, he led us all down into the catacombs under the main store. The men each grabbed a one-gallon glass jug from shelves. Then we proceeded under dim hanging bulbs to where the biggest wooden barrel I had ever seen squatted in a corner. A big wooden spigot protruded from it. With a flourish of keys, Ed opened a padlock, pulled the cork from his jug, put the jug's mouth under the spigot, and turned the handle. Red wine gushed forth.

Once he had the jug half-filled, he closed the spigot, wiped off the mouth of the jug with a handkerchief, and handed the jug to the Russian colonel, who with an impressive snap of his heels, bowed, took the jug, put his mouth to it and drank. He nodded his head down in approval and handed the jug to Clausen. Ed wiped again with the hanky and drank. Then the White Russian drank and finally my dad. I alone went dry. The men filled the other jugs, taking a pull from the first jug now and then, refreshing it as necessary. In a short time, the Russian expedition had four gallons of the best red wine Fairbanks had to offer and the members of the filling party had finished off quite a bit themselves. The N.C. basement was quite merry, except for me. I was hungry. I chafed to go home, knowing that Mom's fury would explode if we were not there when she was ready to set grub on the table.

Dad and I arrived home about eight o'clock, me querulous from low blood sugar and him still merry and psychologically prepared for my mother's black-Irish anger. That fell upon us like a cold mist the moment we entered the cabin. The punishment rained on me as well as on him. I had neglected my duty of warning my mother about what was going on. I was no better than this drunken lout, your father, and so on and so forth.

Brother Buzz wisely kept quiet in a corner.

Twenty

ALTAR BOYS

Shortly after my First Communion, one of the Jesuit priests at the Church of the Immaculate Conception asked my mother to enroll me in a new afternoon class for altar boys.

Mom was thrilled, she told me when informed of this honor awaiting her firstborn. "But don't tell Dad, not yet," she said, "I'll do that."

I didn't need it explained that my dad disliked organized religion. He had no religion except that of worshiping the outdoors. Without my mom around, he scoffed at the idea that there existed some great gray-bearded white gent treading clouds with sandals and staff, dispensing goods and evils to earth's mewling bipeds. Dad kept a complete set of Mark Twain's works that he read and reread when he wasn't engrossed in *True Detective* and other magazines featuring gory pictures and lurid crime writing. Mark Twain, he said, provided enough laughs and ideas to sustain a whole civilization.

In the classes conducted in the church's cold, barren basement, priests set us sprats to memorizing the Latin responses of the low mass. I didn't have the slightest idea what the words meant. We learned them by rote. A priest would declaim the lines that a priest would say or chant. Our soprano and alto voices piped back the responses. We also practiced chanting in Latin.

Playing around in these classes, talking out of turn, not paying attention, or dozing resulted in that great freshener of the mind, that concentrator of intellect—the priestly punch, usually a backhand delivered across an ear, though one rotund reverend used a variation that truly increased attention. He would call an errant boy forward to stand with a stiff spine, hands dangling. Then, the good Father would step forward with cupped palms and slam them together over the ears of the littler sinner. The clap thundered into the ears. Worse, compressed air slammed the ear drums. It hurt like hell. But if you sniveled or cried, he'd do it again. After I fell victim to my first attack of the thunder clap, I complained to my mother, who snapped that it was my fault, that the priests know best and whatever they do is all right, and you'd better do it, thank you very much.

Once responses and chants stuck in our brains, we rehearsed in practice masses at the altar or in masses just for nuns, all under the tutelage of one teacher while another priest actually said the mass. We learned when to genuflect, when to bow, when to ring the bell, when to swing the censer spewing incense about, when to fetch the water and the wine, the lighting and carrying of candles, when to turn, when to stand, when to sit, with the priest leading and us servers acting as small chorus. We also trained with senior servers, altar boys well into their teens who had the rank and prestige of being able to serve not just low masses but high masses, too, even when the bishop of Alaska himself showed up to do the honors.

In a few months, we not only served early-morning low masses but also took high-mass response, chant, and positioning lessons. Serving mass is stage acting. Or, at least it was in the days when Pope Pius XII ("a saint on earth"), the small, wizened Italian who made deals with Hitler and Mussolini, presided over the anointed.

I became a star of the altar-boy trade, though what the mass meant or was supposed to mean, both literately and symbolically, I wasn't taught, I didn't know, didn't understand, and didn't care. The training priests stressed that our loyal, devoted, sinless service would rack up positive points in the great account book that God or one of his saints kept to track every individual soul. Positive points would reduce by tens of thousands the years of excruciating but purifying flames we boys would endure in Purgatory if we died in a state of grace—that is, shrived, absolved, forgiven. Of course, if we died in sin, mortal sin as opposed to venial sin, then not even our skilled traipsing through hundreds of masses would reduce our time in Hell by one second. Without being little Pascals or even knowing about the philosopher, we boys acceded to his argument: any Hell-avoidance insurance is better than none.

During my years as an altar boy, I developed a specialty much appreciated by our Jesuit supervisors: appearing angelic and sad at masses for dead children. Children died all the time in those days before antibiotics, few vaccines, and no government help for kids. Two motherless brothers I knew, one my age, whose truck-driver dad liked to beat them when he was drunk and ignore them when he was sober, died from diabetes about a year apart. So far as I could figure in my childish ignorance, they had not received insulin and nobody gave a hoot about them. At the funeral mass each had with a bare spruce coffin, their daddy honked and snorted in the small, screened, candle-lit chapel on one side of the church's nave. This was reserved for family members during funerals. A few nuns in the main church made up the rest of the congregation.

Babies that had not been baptized appeared in little white boxes festooned with hothouse flowers that perfumed the church even before we altar boys lit the incense. The sermons from the priests were always the same, almost word for word, about Limbo on the edge of Hell where the babies souls now floated without joy or pain, hemmed there by the original sin they had not had the time to be washed free of. That forever denied them the presence of God. But God, in his mercy, had prepped this comfortable abode just for them, everlasting. (I cannot express the shock I felt recently when the newspapers reported the new German Pope had, as it were, "disappeared" Limbo because it was not part of Catholic theology. What! What happened to all those baby souls? Transmigration to Heaven? Surely not plunged to Hell? I have promised myself to dive into the new theology of the location of baby souls if I have enough years left for such a swim.)

Appendicitis, scarlet fever, tuberculosis, diabetes, blood poisoning, and undiagnosed ailments harvested small bodies for funeral fodder. So did accidents, commonly known as God's will (a.k.a. the Fickle Finger of Fate), something I was familiar with remembering the drowning of the boy next door, Donny Irwin. A little girl fell onto her head off a ladder her dad had propped against their house. Good-bye. Walter Stock, a classmate, stuck his head out over the gate of the open freight elevator at the N.C. Company, as it rose to the crushing caress of the floor above. So long. A new boy whom I didn't know banged a dynamite cap with a hammer, learning a fatal lesson. Once, we staged a funeral for a child amid whispers about a father or mother's boyfriend whose fists had become deadly weapons when the booze flowed. We sang hosannas over dead children and uttered prayers for the relief of their souls in Purgatory with candles blazing and incense puffing, while behind the black gauze curtain of the side chapel their parents and other kin sobbed, wailed and moaned.

The priests ruled over the altar boys with quick hands. They had to. We were an unruly lot. As we did in school and the streets, we fought with fists over issues of power and prestige in the sacristy. A high honor was helping a priest don his costume before a mass. Even at a low mass, prestige flowed from being the lead piper of Latin responses to the priests' Latin chants. Great distinction accrued to the acolyte who fetched and tendered to the priest the cruets of wine and water necessary for the holy mystery of the mass to occur, that of wine transforming into the blood of Christ and unleavened wafers of bread into Christ's body. We even competed for position in ringing the bell to signal, among other things, the miracle's consummation.

Sometimes handling the wine had a wonderful side benefit, but an altar boy had to take care. Thrifty priests hollered if they saw a draft of sweet altar wine sliding down the gullet of some gangling kid. A parched priest would display hot temper toward an altar boy who beat him to the last swig, especially if that priest wore a hair shirt as part of discipline laid upon him by superiors for drinking too much.

I remember most priests as temperate, humorless souls, who ensured we didn't swipe the wine, checking that we'd put it back in the right bottle, double-checking that we'd stowed the unconsecrated hosts, tidied the altar, and hung up his and our cassocks and surpluses in proper order, in the proper places. Good priests motivated us with praise, milk, and cookies after a particularly trying morning of a high mass with the bishop missing his cues and the rest of us having to wing it until we could synchronize our chants again and proceed in good order.

I cannot remember anyone ever warning me, Jack, be nimble, Jack, be quick, around priests with wandering hands.

But I was nimble and so were the other altar boys. It was a given that behind the altar, as out in the larger society, some men liked to cup your butt or tug your pecker through your pants, all in high spirits, of course. It was considered bad form to yelp about this, just as it was considered stupid to submit and clumsy to become cornered. Never in my career as an altar boy did anyone accuse a priest of "wanting to go all the way," as these matters were put politely, but we did scamper when a priest felt playful.

For me, the low point came in the form of a Jesuit who appeared one day, a tall, scrawny man with food stains on his vest, who loved to pinch. By pinch, I mean with sharp fingernails that grabbed your flesh wherever it offered and held on and dug in, while you writhed in pain. Because we altar boys considered it cowardly to cry out, for a few weeks this bastard enjoyed his pleasures among us, inflicting hurt without anyone telling other priests or parents. Finally we began talking. I had black and blue marks on an upper arm after he nailed me one day. So did others. We talked about him between services when we snuck outdoors, when weather allowed, to cop a smoke behind the bushes. At last this sadist made a serious error. He grabbed the ass of—I'll call him "B"—and squeezed his nails in so hard that he broke B's skin. B was not amused. He was in early adolescence, a boy of brains and guts. We must get him, he said. We agreed.

The opportunity came and B took it. When the priest cut in front of B at the top of the long flight of stairs down from the sacristy, B reared back and kicked the priest in the spine. Our tormentor tumbled bang, bang, bang, crunch. I swear we could hear the bones break as he fell all the way to the lower landing. Instantly we all scattered. I ran as fast as I could back through the sacristy into the church, down a side aisle past a confessional box, into the foyer, and then out into the yard and on Cushman Street and home. I thought the priest was dead or dying.

I never told anyone what happened, nor did any of the other altar boys. Silence blanketed the event. We learned that the father was taken next door to the hospital, where he lay in bed in the plaster casts used in those times to set broken bones while they mended. I saw him the next time I went into the hospital to sell papers. He looked like wax. I did not acknowledge him. He did not acknowledge me. Not long after, he went away, perhaps to new parish hunting grounds.

Ass-grabbing by some of the other priests stopped. The lesson was clear: screw with those altar boys, and they will screw you.

Twenty-one

NATIVES

Dad arrived home early from work on a Saturday just before Christmas. It was cold and clear and the early moon was flooding Fairbanks with a silver glow. Dad hefted onto the kitchen table two brown paper shopping bags bulging with oranges, a rare winter treat during World War II.

Mom clucked with delight. She sorted the oranges onto the table. Buzz and I hovered, slavering. We knew that if the fruits were half frozen, we'd have to eat them in a hurry. Frozen parts would blacken once they thawed. If totally frozen, into the meat grinder they'd go to be pulped and kept frozen until my mom could use the pulp for mixing with seltzer water to create a slushy drink or for mixing with wild cranberries she'd canned to make compote to accompany moose, caribou, mountain sheep, ducks, geese, or grouse.

During the war, N.C. and other grocers freighted fruit to Fairbanks by ship from Seattle to Seward, then by rail from

Seward to Fairbanks. Likewise they imported such perishables as eggs year-round, because local farmers could not supply enough eggs even in summer. The Army snapped up nearly all of summer's fresh produce. Local dairies supplied fresh milk in the spring, summer, and fall, but the supply receded in the winter when the cattle went on short rations, chiefly silage. Fresh milk wouldn't last the weeks-long trip from Seattle. In winter, mothers forced down the gullets of protesting offspring chalky powdered milk mixed with Fairbanks' foul ferric well water. As for fruit, our subarctic summers did not provide enough growing season for even hardy apples. Fresh citrus, apples, pears, peaches, cherries, apricots, and melons were expensive imports.

Even so, my parents bought them because President Franklin D. Roosevelt's New Deal public-health programs stressed the necessity of eating citrus and other fruits and vegetables with vitamin C to ward off scurvy. Scurvy, beriberi, and rickets were commonplace in America among the ignorant and poor. Public campaigns stressed the need to feed fruits and vegetables to youngsters to ward off these crippling and killing diseases. Such warnings today reverberate strangely because few have even heard of diseases causing teeth to fall out, bones to turn to butter, nerves to short circuit, and hearts to fail. Even so, I remember kids in my classes who entered Main School with one or two or all of these savage ailments. Teachers and the school nurse handed out vitamins, vitamin-fortified milk and fruit, raw carrots, and the dreaded doses of cod liver oil. Not only did Mom worry aloud about Buzz and me getting the right grub into our bellies, she also forced us to down what she thought necessary for our survival, causing not altogether happy dining experiences.

However, she did not have to force oranges upon Buzz or me. As soon as we could that evening, we peeled and chomped down slices of those delightful oranges. These were not today's large, heavy-skinned, easily peeled oranges. These oranges, the size of baseballs, carried skins that stuck to their flesh except under the attack of sharp, patient fingernails.

Due to the cost, the de Yonges did not buy oranges often. This day, Dad and some other N.C. employees had salvaged from the store's garbage bins vegetables and fruit good enough to eat but not suitable to sell. Dad trudged home many a day with bags of potatoes, tomatoes—another winter rarity—lettuce, cabbage, and whatever other produce he found. Some had spots and nicks or even rot that Mom and Dad pared away.

The next afternoon, Dad asked me to put on my outdoor duds. He needed help, he said. My mother, meanwhile, had brought in a couple of wooden gasoline-can cases and lined them with old quilts. She covered the linings with butcher paper from the large roll we kept in our new bathroom. Onto these she put bricks heated on our stove and wrapped in old towels. Then, she layered oranges into the boxes, put down another layer of paper, and tucked the rest of the quilts over the tops. My dad lugged the boxes outside and roped them onto our big toboggan, which he and I pulled frequently down onto the Chena River loaded with cans of garbage and buckets of stove ashes to be dumped onto the ice.

You pull first, Dad said, knowing my pride in being able to pull a loaded toboggan.

We set off down Wendell toward town, but turned off onto the stub of Dunkel Street that dead-ended in the willows along the Chena. He turned in at a log house that I knew too well, the home of Fred and Mina Pease. This surprised me. Fred was a big clumsy boy with slow wits that we kids teased and tormented until Fred angered and gave chase. For some years, this sport amused us, especially in the summer when a dozen or more of us hung around the public ballpark just across the street from the Pease house. But the fall previous, just before school started, some of us were circling around Fred, snatching at his clothes and calling him a dummy and worse, when Fred flushed scarlet, grabbed a baseball bat off a rack, and started toward me—at least I thought I was his target—with a look that said he intended to liquefy my brains. We ran for our lives. To my relief, Fred chased someone else, his bat swishing. The rest of us, valorous as we were, retreated to our homes.

I had learned the lesson: don't screw with Fred anymore. I mulled this elementary precept when my dad knocked at the door. It opened a crack.

"Mrs. Pease," Dad said, "we have a bunch of oranges still good to eat that we can't eat. Eva and I wondered if you and your family would want some."

While he talked, I peeked around him and beyond Mrs. Pease, looking for Fred. No sign of him. Dad's offer was accepted.

"Good," he said, unstrapping a case. Suddenly, Fred appeared from the icy mist pouring into the log cabin, accepted the box, stared at me, and shut the door.

(Mina Pease, who also suffered abuse from us smart asses because she was Fred's sister, and because her family was poorer than ours, excelled in school. She became a high-ranking official of the United Nations Association in Manhattan. I have no idea what happened to Fred. If he and Mina still live, I beg them to forgive my ignorant and savage boyish ways.)

Dad took over the toboggan rope. Next, we stopped at a small, slumping log cabin on First Avenue. The cabin door stood under a roof overhang so low my dad had to stoop to knock on the door. An Indian lady in a blue and white calico dress pulled over a moose hide skirt opened the door and looked out. I could smell a baby.

My dad introduced us and offered the oranges. He reached into the remaining box to show what he was talking about. The Indian lady nodded. He unstrapped the box and carried it inside. I followed him into the one-room cabin, which was stifling from the heat of a wood stove in the corner. On a low table flickered a stump of a candle waxed onto a tin plate. There was no sink. Against the far wall, a naked baby slept on a fur spread on a cot. A black-haired boy, his face drained of color, lay on a cot next to the cabin's only window. The boy looked to be about my age, but I didn't know him. He never looked at us. He coughed and coughed again. Then he rolled his head over to the side of the bed and spit blood into a Hills Brothers coffee can on the floor. I wanted to run.

Dad set the oranges next to the table, took out an orange, produced his jack knife, cut through the orange, and handed half of it to the Indian lady. Then he bit into his half. She bit into hers, in imitation. Good for the boy, Dad said, pointing to the sick boy. Dad squeezed his half of the orange and held it up so that juice ran into his mouth. He pointed at the baby. Good, he said, very good. The woman nodded.

I feared to breathe. At school, we'd watched the same movie, year after year, about the dangers of tuberculosis. Many kids had it. When their TB became obvious, they were sent home, never to return. I knew I could catch TB just by breathing in the cabin.

"Don't tell your mother," Dad said after we were back out on the street. "Or she'll get mad as hell at both of us, especially me."

"I won't," I said, and I didn't.

Over the next couple of years, I went with my dad a half-dozen times with fruit and other produce to the homes of families poorer than ours—whites, Indians, Eskimos, all much poorer than ours. Each time he dropped off the food, we left. That was it. Socially, as a family, we had no relationships with Natives, the general term applied in Alaska to the indigenous people we whites found living in Alaska when we showed up with guns and swords and reputations—widespread in what lawyers call Indian Country—for slaughtering any Natives who opposed us. Word of mouth among Native peoples had carried news all the way into the Yukon from the Indian killing grounds east and west of the Mississippi River.

Dad knew many Natives. Native men came into the store to deal with him when he was the N.C. Company's fur-buyer.

The Native and white trappers showed up in the late spring and early summer with bales of beaver pelts stretched into circles, and of stretched fox, martin, wolverine, mink, and ermine skins. Fur-buying was a handshake business, based on skill and trust. Dad would approach a bale of beaver pelts, say, and run his fingers over the top pelt and then over the bottom pelt. The best pelt was on top, the worst on the bottom. His fingers then counted the pelts. He offered a price for the whole bale. Usually, the trapper nodded agreement. Dad would enter the price on a special form. Then he would inspect the next bale of furs, and so on. A trapper might flare each pelt in a bale if he thought they were so good that the bale deserved more than the going price. Dad would finger each pelt and quote an amount until there was a nod. Many transactions, after my dad had summed all prices he had jotted down, amounted to thousands of dollars at a time when one thousand dollars would buy a new Plymouth, Ford, or Chevrolet.

Once Dad announced the final figure, and the trapper accepted it, they would shake hands. The business was over except for the bookkeeping. In a special book of receipts, each with its own carbon paper, Dad would write a receipt listing the bales for such and such a value. He and the trapper would walk halfway across the N.C. to the business office to give the receipt to a clerk. The trapper would tell the clerk how much cash he wanted, how much credit for purchases. Trappers applied much of their money to their accounts. Dad told me that the cash they folded into their pockets would be spent on whiskey, a room and a bath, a haircut and a shave, and one or more trips to the Whore Line. Shortly thereafter, the smiling trapper would reappear at the N.C., skin glowing, to order another year's outfit—traps, rifle and shotgun cartridges, hardware, dried and canned food, new underwear, and outdoor togs, usually to be freighted to his cabin by bush plane.

Each year in the late summer, our family drove to Graehl, across the Chena from where we lived, where a big family of Indians kept a winter cabin. Hardly anybody would be around except an old woman. The others all were out on the Tanana and the Yukon rivers catching and smoking king and dog salmon and killing moose and other game to be made into jerky. The old lady would measure us for moosehide moccasins, mittens that would come up almost to our armpits, and sometimes jackets for Mom and Dad. Just about when the snow began to fly, the garments would appear at our door, usually carried by a man. They always fit. The leather was soft and supple with a wonderful smell that belied its tanning and softening that included soakings in human urine. Colored beads decorated all our Indian gear with lovely designs.

Three problems came with this light, comfortable winter gear. Other kids made fun of it. Indian-made was for white trash. Teachers wouldn't let us wear the excellent moccasins in school because they made our feet sweat. Also, given a chance, dogs would chew up and eat these garments. Spot once snacked on one of my mother's beautifully beaded moccasins and received a demonstration of her broom that caused him to shy away from anything Indian-tanned for the rest of his days.

In school, Indian and Eskimo kids—few as there were—supplied targets for our endemic prejudices. I remember no black or Asian children in the concrete confines of Fairbanks' only school. The handfuls of Native children came and went, none staying for long, feeding that inborn human desire to ostracize and punish those who were different than our kind. Racism was legal under state and federal law and was embedded in the culture of the day of "The Greatest Generation."

At home, Mom warned us to stay away from Native children because they were dirty and diseased, even those attending masses at the Catholic Church, sitting in the back pews. My father had a different view, I think, but he had reached an age where he found peace with my mother to be more rewarding than contradicting her, the latter producing only brimstone. Neither he nor she ever said what I heard other adults say often, that Jews were dirty and had diseases and would cheat you any chance they got. The Liebes, my father's in-laws via the marriages of his sisters Dora and Etta, were descendents of a pioneer Oregon family whose patriarch had helped found the Columbia River community of The Dalles and who had become one of Oregon's chief merchants and politicians. Many of my father's friends were Jewish, and one, Bill Sherrod, for many years ran with a partner a haberdashery on First Avenue. Dad wept when Sherrod fell over dead.

Thus, my brother and I grew up without catching the anti-Jewish virulence that during our formative years caused Hitler and his thugs to slaughter approximately six million Jews during World War II.

We did share in the wartime's widespread hatred of Japanese, however. I cannot remember any Japanese-Americans in Fairbanks during my boyhood. Perhaps our government, in its national spasm of fear-fed racism sanctioned by Roosevelt and upheld by the U.S. Supreme Court, already had carted them all off, including children, to concentration camps. That crime against Japanese-Americans happened elsewhere in Alaska, including the Aleutian Islands, where our Army ran off many Aleuts at the point of a bayonet.

No one ever mentioned that while Alaska was a territory under the control of the U.S. Department of the Interior—then, as now, setting governmental standards for backwardness and corruption—Uncle Sam would tear Native children from their families to send them off to Indian schools often thousands of miles away. The department's Bureau of Indian Affairs, threatening arrest if necessary, placed the youngsters in the care of keepers—often protestant missionaries—who herded them to distant boarding schools to become "improved" Natives acculturated to become like Dick and Jane, to become brown-skinned white people. Teachers punished students for speaking their native languages. Students ran away, ignorant of how difficult it would be to get back to their families and their homes. U.S. marshals chased them down and brought them back.

In the dormitories, run by characters inspired by the workhouse characters in *Oliver Twist*, existence was governed by rigid discipline and regimented schedules for everything from taking a leak to eating breakfast. The boozing such institutions piously intended to prevent in fact flourished. So did bullying and fighting among children from different Native cultures that had been warring with each other for eons. I never heard an adult say this was a bad thing.

In school, we pegged the Native kids as not only inferior and stupid in part because they spoke guttural English with funny accents. We also associated these children with drunken Indians we saw lying in the gutters next to downtown dive bars (next to the white drunks) who were swept up by town policemen every morning. Their names were the source of great amusement—John Joe, Joe John, Peter Paul, Mary Sarah, and Sarah Mary, to name a few. We did not know that white missionaries and federal functionaries had hung these names on them. Traditional Native names were too hard to spell and too hard to pronounce. Suddenly, even the newborns were given birth certificates with simplified and simple-minded monikers stamped on them.

We white kids also brought from home the quaint, not yet vanquished American notion that equated one's value with the amount of "white blood" that flowed through the veins of a kid otherwise classified as nonwhite. Adults talked about breeds:

Half-breeds, quarter-breeds (sometimes quadroons), and eighth-breeds (often octoroons). Because many of the leading male pioneers of Alaska, whatever their racial prejudices, never hesitated to unbutton their trousers to couple with a Native woman, many part-white, part-Native students came and went in Fairbanks. Some mixed-race children, by virtue of having sufficient white genes, escaped being dragooned into distant boarding schools.

We tormented these kids without mercy, and occasionally paid for our behavior. One day in eighth grade, I made a snide comment to John John, a husky lad who recently had appeared. In response, John said he would be waiting for me outdoors after school, and he said this loudly enough that soon everyone knew about his challenge. I could neither ignore him nor escape. The prospect of a fight after school was greeted with gleeful anticipation. John John and I had a guaranteed audience. Bets would flow.

It was a sunny, brisk March afternoon. Snow and ice covered the ground. John John waited for me across Eighth Avenue from the school grounds. Twenty or thirty kids, mostly boys, gathered eagerly to watch. John and I both wore schoolboy affectations of the day—calf-high logger's boots with steel toe caps, thick leather soles and heavy elevated heels, good for kicking in an opponent's ribs.

We stowed coats and mitts, squared off, but did not follow the Marquess of Queensberry boxing rules. John punched me hard, under the breast. I fisted his cheek, missing his nose. Soon I was bleeding from the nose and a split lip, he from a mashed lip. Then I slipped and rolled. His kick glanced off my shoulder blades. I lunged to avoid his next kick, grabbing his ankle and pulling. Down he smacked. I grappled him. To cheers and shouts we rolled, gouged, bit, and kneed. Then, we managed to get up and exchange more blows. I harbored a strange feeling: John John was a good fighter, an equal. So I hit him twice as hard as he had hit me.

For the next twenty minutes, we battled out onto Cushman Street and down the street toward downtown. Our audience grew. Cars stopped. Men joined the cheering and placed bets. Across from City Hall, bone weary, we staggered to stay on our feet. I worried about what my mother would do when she saw my torn, bloodied clothes. Firemen from the fire station next to City Hall came out. One of them waded through the crowd, grabbed John and me by our shirts, and pulled us apart. I worried that when he released me, I would collapse, exhausted. He dragged us into the station's bathroom and ordered us to wash up. We looked like pigs. I looked at John. He regarded me. I stared in the mirror. I looked just like he did—swollen face, bubbling nose, split lips, bruises already coloring. I would catch hell at home.

Without speaking, John and I washed in a sink big enough for a dozen men to wash at once.

Go home, the fireman said, don't fight again. If you do, I'll hear about it and drag you home myself and tell your mothers to whip hell out of you.

Our audience had vanished. We walked together without speaking to retrieve our coats, shivering and let down. I caught verbal hell from Mom at home and a generous application of painful iodine. My old man wasn't happy either: there had been no clear victory by his son.

Later, John John stopped coming to school. I have no idea what happened to him. Maybe the marshals grabbed him and he was sent off to boarding school.

As for me, I acquired a deep respect for the Native kids and left them alone, not because I suddenly had become an angel, or had been visited by one, but because, if nothing else, I felt that making someone else miserable would not make me feel any better. It was not worth it.

This was not a moral position so much as moral exhaustion.

Twenty-two

PRO STATION

School ended in late May. By then, the sun was high, the air warm. Robins chortled. Swallows dived and twitted. Peeping leaves greened the birch, aspen, and cottonwood. Pollen and dust from drying streets perfumed the air. The lust for baseball soon followed.

Fairbanks had two baseball fields, both by the river next to the town's only swimming pool, at the lower end of Noble Street. Griffin Park, the big ballpark, hosted the amateur and semi-pro civilian teams, Junior League teams for adolescents, and military teams, many featuring former major-league players. The adjacent ballpark for kids covered a chunk of the town's only formal playground, a sandy place offering a few swings, a slide, horseshoe pits, climbing ropes, parallel bars, and a push carousel. When we were bored, we kids sometimes whirled some unsuspecting victim around on the carousel—

faster and faster, never letting up—until they became drunk, and then sick, with dizziness. Ah, the simple pleasures of youth.

The playground had a shack for storing bats, balls, and other sports equipment. Inside along the walls were short, deeply carved wooden benches, a stove, and a desk lighted by a single bulb dangling from the ceiling.

Doc Shields presided here each summer. He was a high school teacher who in his later years resembled President Harry Truman. Or, rather, I decided Harry Truman looked like Doc Shields. The town paid Doc a few pence to keep the playground running peacefully and to scare off the buggers as we called child-molesters. We had other good Anglo-Saxon names for those men, as well, names then as now eschewed by the genteel. Doc taught us baseball and such pickup baseball games as Work Up, which allowed a miscellany of whatever youngsters showed up to work their way up from right field to center field to left field to third base and then to shortstop, second base, first base, catcher, pitcher and thence to batter, through outing batters and runners in the conventional ways. Initial positions we arrived at by lot, with great disputes centering on who would umpire. That an umpire would favor his friends was a given. Doc frowned upon favoritism, preaching to us about "sportsmanship," a concept foreign to boys who organized themselves by neighborhoods, clans, and tribes for the simple purpose of beating up one's enemies. Still, when he talked about being a good sport to those who weren't, Doc glowed with enthusiasm.

The kids' ball field doubled as practice field for Junior League, played by youths twelve and older. Among these was my baseball and fisticuff hero, Hartley Hansen, a boy who looked like a man with his narrow hips, wide shoulders, muscled legs and arms, and strong frame. None among us doubted that for his age, Hartley was our town's toughest hombre. When someone challenged Hartley, the news electrified us. When Hartley punched, bones and teeth crunched. Only those much older and bigger could whip Hartley, who had begun shaving by eighth grade, and even then not without suffering considerable punishment. Hartley never ducked a fight.

None among us neared Hartley's speed, grace, and strength. When he swung, his ash bat lashed against baseballs with a crack, frequently drilling the ball into the Chena River. Hartley fielded with speed and ease. He could arm a baseball from center field to home plate in a straight line no more than four or five feet off the ground.

One sunny day, Doc Shields was pitching batting practice in the kids' ballpark. The crack of Hartley's bat kept the outfielders busy chasing his line drives. It was a day warm, overcast, heavy with the smell of grass and river mud.

When a convoy of Army trucks rumbled onto left field, we quickly lost interest in batting practice. A bulldozer snorting diesel smoke clanked off of a trailer. Surveyors with transits spread out. GIs in fatigues clambered out of canvas-topped trucks. One truck disgorged shovels, picks, and other tools. Another arrived with peeled, varnished, and notched spruce logs. The U.S. Army's construction engineers, we learned, had invaded a big chunk of left field to build a big, single-story log building where Lacey Street ended at the river.

We flocked over to beg candy and cigarettes. GIs tossed us Mars bars hard as rocks. Most of all, we begged for Camels and Chesterfields and Lucky Strikes ("Not a Cough in a Carload") in five-cig packs that the patriotic tobacco companies donated to our fighting men, addicting them to nicotine for the rest of their lives. We smoked only when Doc Shields retreated inside his shack. He had the power as an official adult to seize our smokes and sermonized at length against the evils of tobacco. Aside from smoking, we valued cigarettes as trade goods. I could barter a packet of smokes for two, maybe three, well-read comic books. This was important because I spent much of my time devouring comics—this was my intellectual life—and figuring out how to acquire more with little or no money.

We wondered what all the construction was about. "Damned if I know, kid," one private told me as he leaned on the handle of a shovel. "I hear it's for clap."

Given my early instinct for news-gathering, I delighted in relating to my friends that the construction was for the "clap and the blue balls too," as one popular ditty went among us. The clap, syphilis, the blue balls, creeping crud, the sore-nosed dick—we all knew what those were, the very things our priests and ministers and parents and others warned us against once we reached the age when the pleasure of getting was worth more than the pains of getting rid of them.

"Social diseases!" The syllables roll still. "Venereal diseases!" Gonorrhea and syphilis one acquired in ways no one in those puritanical days would specify to us. My mom also warned me about toilet seats, how I had to cover them with toilet paper before I pressed my pure buns upon them. I tried that once and gave up on the experiment. Kissing girls with sores on their lips? Well, the esthetics of sores discouraged desires to mingle labia. As for sexual intercourse, the prudishness of the time sheltered us from any formal or useful knowledge of the lubricious activity upon which the survival of the species depends. I did know, from being forced every year to attend a hellfire lecture by some visiting Jesuit highly trained in frightening children, that if you "played" with your crotch parts, this shameful sin would bring on demons and devils and loathsome diseases far worse than the leprosy. Shortly thereafter I experimented, only to find his assertion not true: no devils and no diseases appeared, at least not yet.

So much for formal knowledge. As for informal knowledge of sex, well, our schoolrooms and hallways and homes brimmed with prurience. Before I was five, the little girl next door persuaded me after she pulled her drawers down to feel between her legs for what my innocent eyes took to be something I had rarely seen—a fresh peach. Then she felt me, and I experienced my first erection. In first grade, some of us would gather at the home of the Hardy boys over at First Avenue and Hall Street for detailed lessons in copulation from girls in our neighborhood. We stripped off our clothes for these orgies of keen interest but little consequence due to the shortage of male gear.

In school, I succumbed to blandishments a number of times before fifth grade from girls interested in viewing and feeling my equipment, usually in cloak rooms. As for chitchat on the subject, we boys engaged in much discussion and speculation that toward sixth or seventh grade blossomed into vast knowledge thanks to the introduction of a daisy deck by Bobby Burglin. A daisy deck of playing cards featured black and white pictures of posed pornography in which naked women and men indulged in sexual gymnastics that to this day fill me with wonder. By the time one had studied all fifty-two cards, nothing much remained to the imagination about what two people could do to, and with, one another, even two people of the same sex. Burglin charged me one dollar for a look-see. I never spent a better dollar for acquiring knowledge.

During summers, we who played or lived near the willows along the Chena had frequent chances to spy on sundry screwing in the thickets. Participants thought they canoodled in privacy. What they didn't know was that Al Baumeister, Burglin, and I had honed skills at being stealthy scouts. We could tiptoe through the willows without cracking a twig. We could snake silently through the willows and grasses on our bellies. What we could not do, I discovered, especially when my brother Buzz became old enough to tag along, was smother our giggles. Many a time when ten or twelve of us would be on our bellies in a circle around a copulating couple, someone would snort or cough, signaling a failing effort to smother a hee-haw. Unfortunately, a titter would burst all restraints, and a fanfare of laughs, cackles, and snorts would follow. Some lubricious couples didn't care and never missed a stroke. Sometimes—oh, beware, beware!—an angry swain would jump up, with fire and murder in his eyes, struggling to pull up shorts and pants. Our covey would flush with shouts and warnings, to reconvene a hundred yards away for panting, back-slapping, and guffawing. After one of these episodes, I learned not to stop running if both lovers were men. When we had two men after us, they seemed fleeter of foot and more filled with fury than just one man who had to abandon a woman to chase us. Different tastes, different results.

Over the next few days, the Army engineers, with a bevy of officers looking on, erected in left field a varnished log building with large windows and a green-tin, sharply pitched roof. Then came trucks with red crosses on the side. The Army Medical Corps took possession and equipped the place. Finally, with MPs taking their posts at the door, it opened for business. It soon became known as the Pro Station.

That evening, as families watched their kids play baseball, young soldiers in dress uniforms and in civvies visited the new building. By the fourth or fifth inning, a line had formed. The man at the head of the line, upon summons, would step forward, present papers to an MP, and be waved in. Another would follow. Sometimes the line would move until ten or fifteen men had gone inside. Then it would stop. After a few minutes one man and then another, some white at the gills, emerged from the back door to board an Army bus. Once it left, another bus would replace it.

On Saturday nights, the lines would be very long and even longer on paydays at month's end. Prophylactics were handed out, we learned, but that wasn't the half of it.

Even unsophisticated tykes like me saw that those going in looked unhappy and those coming out looked worse. Why? We hung around the door until the corpsmen and MPs got used to our presence and paid us no mind when we peeped in or snuck in. What I saw produced one of the strongest memories still illuminating my brain.

As soon as a man stepped inside, holding his identification papers and pass from Ladd Field or 26 Mile and with his metal dog tags hanging out over his chest, he presented himself to a sergeant, who checked the tags against the ID and the pass. The customer then stepped to the next table, unbuttoned his fly to grasp his short arm, as the Army called it, for inspection. He'd unlimber and present his penis.

The corpsman would pick up what looked like a hypodermic syringe and needle big enough to inoculate an elephant. It was a device called a flechette from which, when you compressed the handle, little surgical blades would snap out on the four sides of the end of a long, thin, hollow tube. The tube dripped with lubricant. The corpsman with one rubber-gloved palm would cradle the GI's penis while, with a deft motion, he inserted the tube up the unfortunate's urethra, the penile duct through which both urine and sperm discharge. Then the corpsman would compress the handle. The GI would yelp. The corpsman would draw the flechette out with its blades extended. Blood spurted forth. The corpsman would put a piece of gauze over the end of the penis and instruct its owner, "Grip your dick and go to the next table."

At the next table, the victim would present arms to a corpsman who presided over a tray full of long-needled syringes. He would grasp the bleeding penis, insert a needle up the urethra, and discharge the contents of the syringe—salvarsan, a whitish, arsenic compound used to treat syphilis before penicillin was available.

This injection generally produced a groan of pain from the owner of the invaded organ. The corpsman, ignoring the groans, gave the soldier another swab for cleaning his penile tip and told him to button up and step to the next table. Many proceeded with more of a limp than a step. At the next table, the GI presented his pass, which received a stamp and a scribbled signature from a sergeant, who then pointed to the back door. The ordeal was over, until the next time.

To get back onto Ladd Field or any other military installation, every enlisted man had to present a pass stamped at the Pro Station for the salvarsan treatment, even if he had come to town only to play the organ at church, attend a baseball game, or relax at the United Service Organization (USO) recreation hall.

The order for this treatment came from the next thing to God in Alaska during those war days—Army General Simon Bolivar Buckner Jr., commander of all military in Alaska during the first years of the war.

Buckner was the son of a Confederate general, a graduate of the Virginia Military Institute and West Point, and was commandant of West Point before the war started. He was a racist and a prude, too, according to biographers. He didn't want blacks in his command and treated them accordingly in Alaska, forcing them to live and sleep in tents during the winter, including days when the temperature dropped to fifty degrees below zero. He refused to issue passes to blacks. I heard Buckner cursed by Fairbanks pioneers, as they liked to call themselves, because he ordered the Fairbanks mayor and council to shut down the Whore Line or he'd put all of Fairbanks off limits to the military. His command grieved town fathers because honest profits flowed from both the hookers and the military that flocked to town to carouse and otherwise recreate.

Closing the Fourth Avenue line occurred, ostensibly. Some cribs stayed open, though discreetly. The town's wink-wink order closing the Line populated the bars with town whores by providing them an excuse to spread their business activities farther afield. It also had the grander effect of sprouting a sporting district of whorehouses, bar-girl saloons, massage parlors, pawn shops, and liquor stores in what became known as South Fairbanks along the Richardson Highway south of Gaffney Road and beyond the town's border. Pent-up demand also inspired the opening of satellite dens of good-natured vice—well, not counting a few muggings and holdups—in Graehl and on the Steese Highway near the back gate to Ladd Field.

The geographical redistribution of sex for hire that Buckner stirred also elevated the VD rate, the very thing he wanted to avoid. Artillery fire killed General Buckner in June 1945, on Okinawa, where he commanded U.S. Army forces in that bloody battle with the Japanese.

The nation mourned Buckner's death, and Fairbanks did, too, but with restraint.

Having the Pro Station in left field created problems for Doc Shields, not the least of which were line drives that Hartley Hansen bounced off the building. This was a ground-rule double, Doc decided. Now and then, a ball smashed through one of the windows—a ground-rule home run. When this happened, angry Army staff swarmed forth and those among us with brains ran away laughing toward home.

Official nastiness was Doc's problem to deal with, not ours.

Twenty-three
HARDING LAKE

Warmed by the sun, I awakened to the smell of the birch and the rhythmic sound of waves lapping upon the lakeshore. A breeze rustled the screens on the porch where I lay under a quilt on an old couch, conscious of a glorious July morning. In the distance a loon cried. It was quiet inside, behind the screen door, where Mom and Dad and my brother slept at Hunters' camp—a small summer house that Bill and Maggie Hunter built on stilts just up from the beach at Harding Lake.

Each year, my dad took a week's vacation from his job. As in summers past, we vacationed at Bill and Maggie's camp, near the Clausen camp, the Almquist camp, the Pollock camp, and a dozen others. Most of the lakeshore then was empty, remote, and roadless.

I slipped on shorts, a tee shirt and white, low-cut canvas and rubber Keds. Then, in the shadows of the birch and aspen, I peed off the landing of the stairs leading down to the beach.

Relieved, I entered the kitchen and living area, where my brother slept on a couch under plaid blankets near a windup Victrola. The room smelled of split birch firewood stacked in a wooden box next to the big, white-enameled stove, used for heating as well as cooking. I found some corn bread left from the previous night's supper and a handful of wild strawberries Mom had picked. I pocketed a bottle of 6-12, the new oily, gluey, burn-like-hell-in-a-cut mosquito dope said to be the same stuff the Marines had used on Guadalcanal.

After gulping the cornbread and berries, I hurried out to the red canvas canoe Dad had drawn up onto the dock, rolled it over, and launched it. I loaded two paddles and leaned against the stern our True Temper steel casting rod with its Shakespeare level-wind casting reel. Hooked to the reel's arbor was my dad's plug, the Ruptured Duck, which he had carved out of white spruce, painted fawn tan on the bottom, dark brown on top, and then varnished. On the water, the plug presented the shape and size of a baby mallard. From the plug dangled a treble hook. Dad had honed its three points razor sharp.

I untied the canoe, eased into it, and with one of the ash paddles stroked out onto the lake, turning toward the reeds on the lake's eastern shore. As I paddled along the shoreline, the number of camps thinned until finally there were none, just forest. My passage disturbed a mother mallard. Five ducklings splashed after her, quacking, as she paddled for cover in bulrushes.

I glided the canoe toward a large bed of pickerel reed. No pickerel lived in Harding Lake, but northern pike, the pickerel's big cousin did. (Dad and his friends called the pike pickerel more often than they called them pike.) The sun already stood high in the southeast. The wind puffed from the south. I pivoted the canoe to put the sun on my back so that I could see without glare into the thin reeds and the gold-sand shallows. The water was only a couple of feet deep. My eyes searched indentations in the lines of reeds—little lagoons, Dad called them. I hunted for a torpedo shadow over the sand, a shadow thrown by the pike's mottled green and white body. Ahead, a shadow much longer than wide undulated under the waves. I dropped a small stern anchor and tied off the anchor line once the canoe, pushed by the wind, pointed toward the pike.

As Dad taught me, I concentrated on not making a noise that would spook the pike to dash through the reeds out into deep water. I hefted the rod, unhooked the duckling plug. I took three deep breaths, aimed the plug to drop six or seven feet ahead of the fish, and cast. The plug sailed out. I thumbed the spinning reel to slow, then stopped it. The duckling halted in flight, plopped onto the lake, bobbed there, in the right place. Excited, I swallowed, breathed hard, and fought the urge to move, except for a few turns of the reel handle to wind slack out of the line. As soon as energy from the splash reached it, the shadow turned toward the plug. With the rod tip parallel to the water and pointed at the plug, I tugged the line ever so slightly. The duckling wriggled.

Suddenly, in a surge of water, the pike ripped forward. In a great splash, the false duckling disappeared. I gritted my teeth in excitement and counted: one, two, three . . . the line tightened . . . four, five.

Then I wrenched the rod tip, jamming the hook points into the fish's mouth.

Contact! The lake boiled. The mottled head of the pike, its long jaws full of teeth clamped on the duckling, poked out of the water. Was it hooked? The pike thrashed. Yes! Line whizzed under my thumb, reel handles buzzed, gears zipped as the fish rushed away. The rod bucked.

Transported with excitement, I stood up, maintaining balance with shifting feet. The steel rod sprang back and forth as the fish struggled. I reeled quickly to keep the line tight, but not too tight. A snub could pull the hooks from the pike's hard mouth. Slowly at first, then slightly faster, the line came in. The pike dashed toward the canoe. I reeled frantically. The pike torpedoed under the canoe. The line rubbed the keel. I cursed. I worried that the line would tangle in the anchor rope. Holding the rod with one hand, I sat, grabbed the rope and hoisted the anchor onboard. Sand roiled where the anchor had jerked out of the sand. The canoe sloshed from side to side, floating free. With one-handed paddle strokes, I backed the canoe off the line.

The pike stopped. It lay in the crystal clear water barely finning, the plug dangling from its shut jaws. Its gill covers flapped. It was three feet long. The fish stared at me with large yellow eyes and black pupils, the cold gaze of a hunter sensing death, but not without struggle. The pike was far from exhausted. Despite the pressure I put on it with the deeply bent rod, it resisted and rested, marshaling energy.

I had no net. We never used a net to land a pike. I knew I would need to press both eyes simultaneously with thumb and forefinger, to paralyze the fish, to keep my flesh from being ripped by the pike's razor teeth or by the treble-hook points not embedded in the fish's jaw. When I pressured the pike toward the canoe, the water exploded again, and the pike thrashed and tossed on the surface, rolling and twisting. These were the moves of its end game. One minute the fish's tail showed out of the water, the next minute the head. Suddenly, the line went free, slack. The Ruptured Duck and its hooks sailed right at my nose. I flinched away and barely kept the canoe from capsizing. Ripples wrinkled the lake where the pike had been.

Breathing hard, sweating, tingling, sad but elated, I felt the sadness and happiness of the angler who has just lost a great fish.

I paddled around some more, but I couldn't find any pike big enough to entice me. I returned to the dock. The smell of bacon hung in the air. Over breakfast, I described the battle, with hardly more than fifty percent exaggeration. My mom, who loved fresh pike baked, prayed for better luck next time. Dad nodded, laughed, and commiserated. Over decades he had hooked, landed, and lost hundreds of pike in Harding Lake,

Birch Lake, and Lake Minchumina, where he said he'd hooked and landed a pike five feet long—a pike as long as I was tall, a green monster that surged out of the weeds to attack and gorge on a muskrat or a baby beaver. My toes tingled as I imagined such a monster pike.

Twenty years earlier, Harding Lake, "the Lake," as Fairbanksans called it, showed on maps as Salchakett or Salchaket Lake, named after the band of Athabascan Indians who fished and trapped the lake but lived chiefly near the mouth of the Salcha River, about ten miles to the north. Dad liked to fish the river for grayling and salmon along the bars just upstream from where the Salcha drained its clear, tea-colored water into the Tanana's glacial murk. Many times, Dad took me to the Salcha Indian village nearby. He always brought food and tobacco and sat and smoked and talked with his friends there.

No young people lived at the village, only old people, some barely able to limp around with a thick willow cane. The Great Flu of 1918-19 killed most of the Indians, Dad said. It killed a lot of whites in Fairbanks and on the mining creeks, too, but where it hit the Indians, it nearly wiped them out. They had little resistance to the foreign invaders—tuberculosis, scarlet fever, diphtheria, measles, and whooping cough brought into the country by white people from 1902 onward. The surviving young people abandoned the Salcha village to work in Fairbanks, where many fell foul of booze. Like the Irish, Norwegians, Finns, many Russians, and other genetic sets who in evolutionary terms only recently had come into contact with alcohol, the Natives were easy victims of the new poison. When they drank, natural selection worked upon them in the form of deadly fights, suicides, drowning, freezing to death, car crashes, and other accidents.

When I was selling newspapers, I'd step around comatose Indians and Eskimos and whites on the sidewalks outside of First and Second avenue bars. In the summer, the cops left them alone unless some solid citizen complained. In the winter, police gathered them up and dumped them into the drunk tank at the town jail, a foul cave with a concave concrete floor and a drain in the middle so jailers could hose the place down to wash away the urine, puke, and other leavings from the poor souls.

On one village visit, Dad told me to take a good look. He pointed to an old cabin built with upright rather than horizontal logs. In front of the door, an old man sat hunched on a wooden box. The cabin's sod roof had small trees and grasses growing out of it. It had no windows. A faded totem pole lay in the grass beside the cabin. He'll die soon, Dad said, he's old and sick and doesn't have any money. He's the chief. Someday nothing will be here.

Years later I went back. I could hardly find where the village had been amid the forest. I poked through the weeds and found old logs and bits of things, but everything else was gone, including the people. The last Salchakett speaker, Betsy Barnabas, died in 1986, one hundred years after the Salchaketts first looked upon a white man.

In 1923, reflecting national sadness, Alaskans changed the lake's name to Harding Lake to honor President Warren G. Harding, who had died in San Francisco two weeks after visiting Fairbanks. Dad said Harding died from helping to drink up all the available illegal hooch in Fairbanks, no small amount during Prohibition.

Prohibition had become national law three years before. Harding, in the midst of bribery and thievery scandals wracking his "Ohio Gang" administration, decided to become the first President to visit Alaska, where he drove the golden spike signifying completion of the Alaska railroad at a July ceremony at the village of Nenana, southwest of Fairbanks. Harding had been a newspaper publisher, an occupation that alone ought to have warned the citizenry of his thirsts and lusts.

Handsome, with a robust speaking voice, a predilection for sex with friends' wives, and an ability to mangle the English language unequaled in the White House until George W. Bush arrived, Harding came north with an entourage that included his ambitious but ailing wife; Herbert Hoover, his secretary of commerce and a future president; and sundry other cabinet officers escaping Washington, D.C.'s heat—figuratively and literally—in the days before air conditioning. Others included his poker and drinking buddies, reporters, and a few Secret Service agents who, according to some memoirs, spent much of their time saving Harding from himself. After nightly poker games that continued into the wee hours at the White House, the President frequently led his pals to a fancy Washington, D.C. whorehouse for additional entertainment. It was said that in a White House broom closet Harding sired a daughter whom later he refused to recognize.

The President's arrival in frontier Fairbanks in 1923 turned the town's citizens out in their finest to celebrate the great man, Dad said. Harding did not disappoint, giving speeches and taking part in various events. Nor did Fairbanks disappoint Harding. Prohibition had spurred townspeople to construct stills and to import corn and rye for mash, bottling machines, even stick-on labels to civilize the product. The bootleg served the President was the good stuff, having been aged at least one week. Harding, Dad said, downed it with gusto. Upon leaving Fairbanks a couple of days later, the Harding expedition drank its way south to the seaport of Seward on his special train. Harding took ill in Seattle, some say. Others believe he became ill on the train to San Francisco. There, he died of a heart attack, or a stroke, or a bad liver, or even perhaps of poison—such were the reports of the day.

However, my dad was sure the main contributing factor were the residual properties of Fairbanks hooch, which he said was never at its finest until you strained out the dead flies through a bandana.

Twenty-four

MR. BEAN

My friends and I talked about physical violence all the time. We expected to see it, experience it, and inflict it.

American society then, as now, doted on violence. At the movies, we watched Hopalong Cassidy shoot down the bad guys in black hats and John Wayne take revenge on the Japs. On the radio, the Green Hornet went after the crooks. Our comics? Well, Captain America used his weight lifter's muscles to punch out the Red Skull and other fascist villains. *Life* and *Look* magazines showed us grinning corpses hanging out of the turrets of blasted German tanks on the Russian front or hanging from nooses dangling from tree limbs where good American white folks, usually Southern but not always, had lynched a black or Jew, even a Catholic now and then. People writhing in electric chairs? Common pictorial fare. We looked at pictures of violence all the time, in our newspapers and magazines.

Boxing? We glued ourselves to radios to hear if finally some white man would whip Joe Louis. And local bouts? Right there in the Fairbanks ballpark, with a ring put up in the infield, with folding metal chairs ranged about, with the cheap seats in the ballpark grandstands, boxing gloves whacked and blood spattered to cheers from the crowd. Al Baumeister and I snuck into the fights one summer evening. We figured paying to see outdoor entertainment was one of the stupidest sins a boy could commit. Weaseling ourselves right up to ringside, we watched men slug each other unconscious or into bloody pulp.

Likely as not, an adult earned praise—not arrest or a lawsuit—for smacking a kid to administer discipline or punishment for such evil doings as sassing back or swiping a cigarette. In school, there was the paddle. One day while I was paying attention to Miss Brown for once, Ronnie Hardy pulled back a big rubber band around which he had inserted the V of a paper spit-wad and let fly. The wad, no insignificant missile, hit me right beside the eye. It stung like a yellow jacket. I yelped. Miss Brown chastised me and wondered what I was doing and why. The code that governed me and any other boys who wanted respect, if only to be free from bullying, required that I say nothing. I already had palmed the wet wad, made by folding and refolding pulp tablet paper, then squeezing it into a V. You put the wad in your mouth to soak it with spit. This gave it weight. Ronnie would receive the revenge I not only desired but under the code was obliged to administer.

Having a father working in the N.C. hardware department gave me access to weapon makings. I never stole from the N.C. That would have shamed my father, a risk too great to take. I always paid for the lengths of glass boiler tubing I used as bean shooters; for the lengths of heavy rawhide I wove into whips or used for slings of the kind David used to tumble Goliath; for the inner tubes to cut for slingshots; and for heavy iron staples used by carpenters, plumbers, pipefitters and others. As the skin beside my eye blackened from Hardy's spitwad, I yenned for my chance. It came a few days later when Miss Brown turned away to write on the blackboard. I inserted a sharpened iron staple into a heavy rubber band, waited until Ronnie turned away, pulled back, and let fly. The staple points sunk into Ronnie's ear. He yowled and jumped up. Blood dribbled from the wound. Miss Brown and my classmates jumped with surprise. Then Ronnie violated the code. He blurted, "Jack did it! Jack did it!" and held up the staple he'd pulled from his ear.

Miss Brown had no choice. From my smirk—I was all but bowing to an admiring audience—she knew I was the villain. She grabbed me, shook me, and dragged me into the cloakroom.

"Did you do that?" she demanded.

"Yes," I said.

"Give me the staples and the rubber band," she demanded. She was familiar with the weaponry of the day. I handed mine over.

"Pull down your pants," she said.

As I did, she went to a locker, opened it with a key, and removed a standard piece of equipment during my grade school days in Fairbanks—a wooden paddle. Rumor had it the high-school shop class made them.

"Turn around," she ordered. "Grab your ankles."

I did. WHAP! Jesus, it hurts, but I mustn't cry, I thought. WHAP! That hurt worse. I sniffed back my tears. WHAP! That really hurt.

"Do you promise never to do that again in school? Do you?" Her voice was imperious.

"Yes, yes."

"Get dressed and follow me." Carrying the paddle, she led me to the front of the room before the sea of delighted, expectant faces scrutinizing me. My buns burned. I was still squeezing back tears. I saw Hardy whispering to a girl, with his eyes on me. While Miss Brown was explaining what evil I had done, and that Ronnie could have been mortally wounded, I signaled Ronnie that I intended to kill him as soon as I could catch him.

The worst part came next. "Apologize to Ronnie," Miss Brown said. "Apologize loudly, NOW!"

"I apologize," I said, holding up an X with my index and middle fingers. The class roared with laughter. By the time the teacher looked to see what I was doing, I had uncrossed my fingers and was standing like a proper penitent.

"He doesn't mean it!" Ronnie exclaimed.

Before he could go further, Miss Brown shut him up. All in all, she was a fair person, and wanted no more of this to go on in class. She knew, I knew, Hardy knew, and everyone knew that the news of my spanking with all the details would rocket through school before the end of the next recess.

I look back on all this now and think of it as the Day of the Smart Ass Revenge. Being a smart ass—I had developed into such a low creature—had paid psychic dividends. That burst of laughter that I evoked had, I felt, injured Hardy worse than anything my fists might do. He avoided me for days. I didn't get a chance to beat him up for nearly a week. That settled our score. He became a friend and ally again.

Every teacher I had in grade school, with the exception of Mr. Bean in eighth grade, taught me a lot, seemed fair, and remained worthy of my respect after all these years. Mr. Bean stood out as different.

We all knew that parents hit their children because we talked about the spankings and beatings we got. I got whacked and my brother got whacked by our mother. But we were never beaten. There was a big difference. We all knew kids whose parents, usually their fathers, beat them. We knew kids whose dads beat their mothers, too. A man beating his wife, well, it was frowned upon then and for a good time later, but it was not illegal, unless the lout managed to kill her. As long as someone used only fists and feet on a member of his own family, that was all right. The law didn't become concerned unless he—and occasionally she—used a knife or a gun.

I remember Billy Latta coming to school with a face black and blue. His dad had become angry with him after Billy's brother died from diabetes, and after paying for the funeral. Short of money, his old man had lost his temper when Billy broke some dishes. Teachers summoned the school nurse, who took a look at Billy's face and gave him aspirin and a hug. I gave Billy a Camel cigarette from Army rations I lifted from an Army truck parked near the Prophylactic Station. Nobody reached for the phone to call the cops.

Mr. Bean delighted in telling his classes how tough he was. He was quick to grab and pinch and slap. Some of us were getting big, though not me. Hartley Hansen, my baseball hero and friend, the toughest of us all, had grown into a handsome, well-muscled young man. He already had a reputation. His father had tried to knock hell out of Hartley one day but, instead, Hartley knocked hell out of his father, causing his old man to ship Hartley to a relative in Seattle for a while, as I remember. That story got around town fast.

So did Hartley's stories about going down to First and Pine in Seattle, an intersection known even among us rubes in Fairbanks, to sell his body. He described to rapt audiences of boys how you stood in tight pants there, and how cars would drive up, and men would signal you, and you'd bargain with them, and then you'd get into their cars and go park nearby. You had to get the twenty dollars first, he said. Always get the money. Then you let them blow you. Sometimes they'd want you to blow them too, but Hartley said he never did. Twenty dollars! That kind of money would buy you breakfast, lunch, and dinner for a week at the Model Café.

A round-headed, broad-shouldered man in his thirties who liked to wear tight shirts and pants showing his muscles, Mr. Bean began to pick on Hartley in class. Hartley had a hard time reading, but not because he was stupid. I learned later that he probably suffered from dyslexia.

One day, Hartley did something that set off Mr. Bean. The teacher started to shake Hartley by the shoulder. Hartley shrugged him off. Mr. Bean shook harder, with a growl. Hartley shrugged even harder. The class froze in silence. I could hear the saws ripping through boards in the high-school shop class next door. When Mr. Bean put a half hammerlock around Hartley's neck, Hartley jumped up, and the teacher staggered back toward the wall. Hartley turned on him, his big fist cocked. Mr. Bean ordered him to go out into the hallway.

Hartley stopped. Time stood still as he made a decision that would affect his life forever. At last, Hartley turned on his heel and pushed desks aside to get to the door. Report to the superintendent's office, Mr. Bean ordered. Hartley turned and fired a stare of hatred at Mr. Bean, then shook his head and smiled. The door closed behind him. That boy hasn't learned anything, Mr. Bean said, looking around at faces that, at best, were neutral, though many were openly disdainful. We were told to resume our reading. Mr. Bean headed for the superintendent's office to deliver Hartley to his punishment.

However, there was no Hartley to deliver. Rather than suffer expulsion, Hartley had walked out of the school, a self-exile. That had the same effect as expulsion. Hartley never came back.

Mr. Bean, now an object of hatred in the class, had acquired an object of pride—a new Buick Roadmaster sedan, one of the first to reach Fairbanks since the end of the war. Bean parked it on Eighth Avenue where youngsters could admire its polish, immaculate interior, fat whitewall tires and its bright-chrome, shark-tooth grill. Everyone wanted to ride in it, but no one wanted to ride with Mr. Bean.

Some of us discussed inflicting a small revenge on Mr. Bean: pouring sugar into his Buick's gas tank. We had heard that sugar in the gas would gum up the engine, render it useless. No one knew for sure. There was a sure way to find out. Two souls braver than I conducted this experiment when no one was about. Four cubes of sugar, they said, plop, plop. The next day, the Buick failed to appear. Mr. Bean rode to school with another teacher. That day, he had left his smirk at home. He seemed subdued in class.

Revenge was sweet.

Twenty-five

BOY SCOUTS

We subjected anyone our age we thought to be "queer" to vicious gossip, savage taunting, and even physical attacks. Hatred of homosexuality permeated the culture.

These fighting taunts we laid on our victims, innocent or otherwise, and our friends. You could call a friend a cocksucker with an affectionate tone and smile, but otherwise you had to expect a fierce counterattack. One had to be careful, of course. Hartley Hansen could tell me and others in an enthralled audience about his adventures in Seattle taking pay from strange men in cars who pulled down his pants. But to call Hartley queer to his face would have been suicide.

I learned the terms "cocksucking" and "cornholing" and the disdain and dislike for homosexuals almost from the first moment I climbed into the sandbox in kindergarten. Some of the worst fights I had occurred because although I was tall, I also was chubby and had noticeable breasts, which offered handles for calling me queer. Only the drubbings I administered and the drubbings I took without whimper—we all knew homosexuals whimpered—saved me from having to wear the general appellation of sissy or pansy or a half-dozen other demeaning terms of the day. That these prejudices continue today in the United States—indeed, entomb themselves within an ossified political party—speaks to the powers of ignorance.

One day, I learned about Jerry Berry, the Fairbanks Fairy. Bob Burglin, I think, pointed him out to me. He was a short, spare man, light of gait, balding early, who always seemed to have a blue baseball cap on and who resembled a starving Alan Ladd, a movie star of the day. Berry, I learned, served as scoutmaster for a local Boy Scout troop and was a pretty good guy, but you didn't want to be in his tent during a camp-out. He had wandering hands, and more, and there was much speculation about the "more."

As it happened, I joined the Boy Scouts because Burglin and other friends had joined. As a Cub Scout, I had found the rituals to be dreary and the ceremonials ridiculous, a prejudice I still have toward ceremonials and rituals.

However, as a Catholic lad, my religion denied me the social splendors of belonging to the Young Men's Christian Association (YMCA), which was full of limp wrists, as we all knew, or to the DeMolay, reputed to be a society of secrets known only by the elite of the elite. During high school, I did attend a DeMolay gathering in secret, a sin mitigated by my amusement at the absurdities of this Shriner farm team's rites with passwords, darkened chambers, candles, and oaths of loyalty. I could go to church for those.

I also attended several Shrine functions at the Shrine Temple on First Avenue, as a guest of my dad's close friend, Bill

Hunter, the superintendent of the N.C. Power Plant. Mr. Hunter was a big man in all respects and stood huge in the Shrine. He took me to functions to which Shriners brought their sons. I came as his "adopted" son and I not only enjoyed the grub and the elaborate costumes of the members with their fezzes and tassels and sashes sparkling with jewels, but I delighted in shooting billiards in the temple's excellent billiard room. My attendance, of course, racked up sins for me in the eyes of the Catholic Church, which regarded the Shrine and other Masons as the devil's disciples. So, with each bank shot, I bought another twenty thousand years or so of fiery roasting in Purgatory.

One day on the playground I heard something bad had happened to Jerry Berry. Somebody's father had come after him with a baseball bat and a skinning knife. Jerry had gone south—an Alaskan idiom for one who departs town in haste, usually with your money, or your wife, or with fear of being killed or jailed.

I became a tenderfoot Boy Scout complete with uniform. The Scout troop had a new scoutmaster, a young Army sergeant with lots of pizzazz. A couple of other young Army guys served as assistant scoutmasters. The first couple of outings that summer were fun, especially a camping trip out along the Chatanika River at Cripple Creek on the Steese Highway near Leonhard Seppala's cabin.

I tented with Jimmy Growden, one of the brightest students in school and a leading athlete. He was good with his fists, too, but also was a person of such moral splendor that he did not gang up like the rest of us. (Growden became a teacher. He and his young daughter drowned with many others on Good Friday evening in 1964. They were on the dock in Valdez, watching the freighter *Chena* unload, when the Great Alaska Earthquake hit. The dock broke apart, the water jumped and rolled, and the dock and warehouses collapsed into Prince William Sound. Most who had been on the dock drowned, even before a tsunami wave hundreds of feet high devastated Valdez.)

Led by one of the scoutmasters, we hiked and we learned knots, first aid, and how to make fires. We fished for grayling. I hooked the biggest fish because I knew where the Chatanika's pools were near Cripple Creek. We helped prepare and cook the meals and devoured them. At night, we sat around a huge campfire and sang. Our scoutmasters seemed especially merry as they led the singing of everything from "America the Beautiful" to the "Engineers Song" with its chorus titillating to school boys, "We are, we are, we are the engineers. We can, we can demolish forty beers . . . ." We sang long and loud into the night, while coyotes howled nearby. One ditty that still haunts my memory of easy racism of the day was many choruses of "The Darkie Sunday School."

When a scoutmaster blew Taps on a bugle, we dutifully retired to our tents. Soon the smell of cigarettes carefully hidden from adult eyes perfumed the evening. I snuck out to join the evildoers. We ran out of smokes quickly, especially after passing around a pint of vodka, the first I ever tasted. Next, we gathered dried birch and willow leaves, crushed them and rolled them into cigarettes wrapped with toilet paper, an unwise experiment that lead to cacophonic coughing, seared nose hairs, and burnt fingers. A hastily tossed cigarette started a fire that spread to the wall of a large waxed-canvas tent. The blaze sparking in the night brought forth the scoutmasters, growling and swearing. They were not happy. They had "borrowed" the tent from the Army. Replacing it now created a problem that could lodge them in the stockade.

My interest in Boy Scouts rose after that trip, despite rumors that funny things had taken place in the scoutmasters' one-man tents. Each scoutmaster honored a Scout by sharing his tent with him. We quizzed those boys and teased them, accusing them of being "asshole buddies" with the Scout leaders. Denials of wrongdoing were made. However, a few monthly meetings later, we had new scoutmasters and word flew around that some fathers had given our previous scoutmaster a severe beating and warned him that he would be killed if he showed up in town again. My mother grilled me. Word had finally reached her. By habit, I denied everything, though I had nothing to deny.

That winter, we had yet another new scoutmaster, who announced that our troop would do something special: during Christmas vacation, we would stage a winter bivouac in Mount McKinley National Park, now Denali National Park. I had winter-camped before with my father.

Our leaders included one of the regional Scout leaders, who showed up in full Scout regalia, which none of us had. We arrived by train at the park hotel on a dark, gloomy afternoon, drove out to the bivouac site in National Park Service trucks, and set up our tents in their headlights. All the while, the temperature kept dropping. We spent a lot of time next to the huge campfire. Dinner turned out to be Army K-Rations, a treat known and detested by millions, including those of us who had stolen them from Army trucks. With us were a couple of super-Scouts—older boys of high rank who, it developed, would take charge of our camp while the adults departed to spend the night at the park hotel. We grumbled about that, figuring they also would have a nice hot meal in the hotel restaurant. They'd be fools not to.

That night, it dropped well below zero. We all shivered and groaned as we lay in our sleeping bags with all our clothes on, including parkas. By one or two in the morning, most of us were standing by the fire, dervishes rotating slowly to turn the side that was burning into the cold and to turn the side that was freezing toward the fire. Morning brought no relief. We ate more K-rations and melted snow for water. Most of us that day would experience constipation, one of the pleasures of a K-ration diet and a virtual certainty when it is so cold only a fool would consider hiking up his parka and dropping his pants and shorts to expose his rear.

Our scoutmasters drove up about noon, full of hearty good cheer and plans for a hike on snowshoes, led of course by the senior Scouts while the big shots remained in camp warming themselves by the fire. When we came back weary from the hike, the adult leaders overdosed us with optimism—one of scouting's prime products. They ate bits of K-rations in solidarity with us, bid us a good night, and headed back to the hotel bar. That became the pattern for three days. On the fourth day, we broke camp and hiked to the hotel, where we wallowed in the heat as we waited for the train home.

My father listened to my tale of this lesson in scouting and told me—"no more. They are a bunch of bastards, the lot of them," he said. I quit attending meetings and sold my Scout uniform.

The lessons from scouting in the park sharpened my eyes as to how things work. I saw that those in power and those with money—usually the same people—handed out hard medicines for the rest of us to swallow while simultaneously exclaiming how good these sour doses were for our moral uplift. From then on, when someone offered me a quaff of uplift, I held onto my wallet and tightened the zipper on my fly. I also saw that the press, especially such magazines as *Reader's Digest* and the *Saturday Evening Post*, presumed to set standards for the world that had little to do with realty. Reality was defined by the white men in charge. Blacks didn't exist in public discourse, unless labeled as criminals. They rioted or made the mistake of provoking white men to lynch them. Indians and Eskimos were scum and drunks, dirty and diseased. Sex? Forget it, unless in marriage. It was never to be discussed. The existence of the Whore Line in the heart of the business district? Well, this was nothing to be talked about in school or in polite settings. We were beating the Japs and Germans, and that's all that counted.

As for homosexuals, they didn't exist. Or, if they did, they were agents of Satan, to be beaten up, arrested, jailed, and, naturally, ridiculed.

The more I saw that the real world did not conform to the establishment propaganda, the more skeptical I became, and remained so. If a man like Soapy Smith offers to sell you for one dollar a bar of soap with a five-dollar bill wrapped around it, run! If someone tells you to pick up a rifle and go kill a bunch of foreigners because honor demands it, make yourself scarce, as my Uncle Finian Delaney did.

The Soapy Smiths rule the world. In some cases, when they enter the room, people stand up and a band plays "Hail to the Chief."

Twenty-six

MY FIRST MOOSE

Dressed in a red mackinaw jacket and red hunting cap, my dad scraped a branch up and down against the rough bark of a spruce tree next to a swamp. I was dressed the same.

"OooooMAH!" my dad called. "OooooMAH!" Then he made another scraping sound with the branch. "OooooMAH!" As he called, I poured water from a canvas bucket onto a rock. We were imitating, we hoped, the sounds of a cow moose in heat, scraping her rear up and down against a tree and peeing mightily between strokes, moaning for a Romeo moose to come satisfy her desires.

We stopped. We listened. Dad especially wanted me to listen. His ears were getting old, he said. I heard the brush move. Something was coming toward us along the edge of the swamp. I nodded and pointed. Dad uttered another amorous moan, as he shouldered his 30.06 and released the safety. I trembled with excitement as I lifted our .30-.30 and eased back the hammer. It snapped into place. I clicked off the safety. "OooohMAH," Dad almost whispered now.

On our left the brush moved again. Dad turned his rifle toward the sound. Suddenly, on our right, a huge, gray bull moose stepped into the clearing. I aimed the Winchester. I waited, expecting Dad to shoot. Hours went by, maybe ten seconds, and then I lined up the front sight of the rifle into the v-notch and aimed for the moose's shoulder. I squeezed the trigger. BANG! I levered another shell into the rifle's chamber. No need to. The bull staggered forward and fell into the swamp.

"Jesus!" Dad said.

I breathed so hard and fast I could barely think. Behind Dad, a cow moose crashed away. But Dad was staring at the bull. A bubble of blood formed on the bull's nostril.

"Christ!" Dad said. "We've got work ahead of us with that son of a bitch in the water. Good shot, though. He was dead before he hit the ground."

I was supposed to be proud, but I felt tired and spent.

We inspected the dead bull.

"Older than I am, tough as tires," Dad joked. "But still frisky enough to come after a cow." Dad clapped me on my back. "You won't forget this," he said. "Let's fetch our packs. We're going to camp here."

We labored all day, a sixty-six-year-old man and a twelve-year-old boy, pulling and pushing that moose out of the mud and water. We gutted it, made a fire, and quartered the moose by flashlight and firelight. We dined on its liver, fried with onion slices. We dozed in the cold September moonlight, feeding the fire to keep bears and wolves away. The next morning, stiff and grumpy, we roasted slices of moose heart for breakfast and drank water from our canteen.

It took all day to pack out the quarters about six hundred feet to where the borrowed pickup sat on an old road off the

Richardson Highway. We barely could wrestle each quarter up into the pickup bed and onto a canvas that Dad folded around the moose meat to keep the blow flies off. By the time we drove off for home in the cool fall afternoon, I could barely move.

Mom greeted us with joy. Bringing home a moose meant we would eat meat that winter. She cooked steaks. We all chewed and chewed and chewed. Buzz gave up. That old moose was tough.

That winter, I shoved frozen hunks of that antique moose into the meat grinder in our shed and cranked the handle. Out came mooseburger for moose loaf, moose meatballs, mooseburgers and minced moose. Somehow, scraps found their way to the floor of the shed where Tip wolfed them down.

"You're going to kill that dog," my dad said one night. "He's so fat he can barely stagger. Stop feeding him moose."

"Yes, sir," I said, winking at Tip. I swear he winked back.

Twenty-seven

MUSIC AND MISS WELLER

Miss Weller, a tall, awkward lady who wore her shiny black hair in a bun, turned the crank on the phonograph next to the blackboard. She put a 78-rpm record on the turntable.

"Many of you have heard this before in *'Fantasia'*," she said. "Remember Mickey Mouse? Helping the sorcerer?"

I imagined Mickey again with his droopy hat and broom. She eased the needle down on the spinning record. The sound of Paul Dukas's little masterpiece came forth. Camille Saint-Saens' "*Dance Macabre*," Igor Stravinsky's "*Rites of Spring*," M. Mussorgsky's "*Night on Bald Mountain*" followed, one each day, all remembered from "*Fantasia*" as Miss Weller told about the music.

Already, I had a taste for classical music, which I listened to occasionally on our Zenith radio. I heard more of it in the

Fairbanks school band, where I played the tuba under the direction of my former cabbage-worm tyrant, Mr. Jacobs.

Rosamund Weller, after whom a school later was named, a leader for decades in bringing first-class classical performers to Fairbanks for subscription concerts, gave me my first opportunity to appreciate classical music as worthy of special care and attention. She nurtured in me a desire for classical music that has sustained my spirits to this day, bless her. An excellent teacher otherwise and later a stellar elementary-school principal, Miss Weller was a bunned angel of western culture. She devoted her professional life to lighting sparks of art in little souls from homes otherwise deaf and blind to the achievements of the civilization in which they lived.

I learned the tuba because I had to. Mr. Jacobs forced it on me. As the school bandmaster and chief music teacher, he needed a tuba player. "You're big enough to carry it," he said. My musical talent was obvious.

The band practiced in the Main School auditorium. I started playing in fifth grade. Other players ranged in age from elementary school students to high-school seniors. We learned marches, including nearly all of John Philip Sousa's marches. We learned band arrangements of classical pieces, including the overtures to "Aida," "The Flying Dutchman," "Martha," and many other operas.

Every year for the high-school commencement, we rehearsed Edward Elgar's "Pomp and Circumstance," playing it over and over as seniors marched in and later, after an hour or so of American oratorical monotony, as they marched onto the stage for their diplomas. This proved almost as boring as the prayers and speeches. Some Protestant divines would uncoil an opening prayer longer than the New Testament, apparently believing that if a yard of prayer was good, a mile of supplication was even better.

We also tooted and drummed and fifed at basketball games, bunching into the bleachers in the school gym. Basketball was a local obsession. The gym would fill with screaming, chanting fans as Chuck Hoyt, Steve Agbaba, Deke Burnette, Cliff Burglin, Jimmy Growden, Al Baumeister, Teddy Wallace, and other heroes raced up and down the floor over the years for Fairbanks High School's blue and gold. The team played whatever team they could find, usually men's league teams or military teams, the latter often salted by former professional players.

Later, I took up the trombone. I tooted third trombone because I never was any good playing it, but even third trombone was more exciting than playing the tuba.

I also played tuba and trombone in the Fairbanks Community Band, which marched and held great concerts. We played with top instrumentalists. I thrilled to hear the town banker, Bill Stroecker, lift his silver trumpet and lead us like Gabriel with a sound so lovely, so quick, so perfect that even memories of the notes issuing from his trumpet's bell evoke in me today a tingle of delight.

Mr. Jacobs also directed the community band. He dragooned me and other student musicians into it because we played instruments the band needed or because a particular student player actually could make a contribution. One such player was Aaron Downing, who played the baritone horn with a beauty surpassed by none.

The Fairbanks Community Band gave concerts in winter and marched with the seasons, especially on Memorial Day, then a holiday celebrated with a great parade, and on the Fourth of July, the greatest summer celebration of all, and not just because it was my birthday. During and after the war, the military furnished bands to march on holidays. Not only did the military bands play well, but they also had uniforms, which we did not, and they could march in step, which we tried to do but with little success despite our enthusiasm.

One winter, William (Billy) Gobracht returned to the community band as conductor. He had founded the band in 1914. Mr. Gobracht I knew because my mother had sent me to him for piano lessons when I was a small boy. He was a Prussian from the old country, a professional coronet player of surpassing excellence, a band and orchestra leader, and a well-known figure in Fairbanks for a half-century.

I first sat with him at the piano at his house. I expected to get from him the same friendly reassurance I had received from a procession of music teachers my mom hired to teach me the piano. Just practice harder, Jackie, they'd say, and of course I agreed, and of course I didn't practice harder, though I practiced hard enough to drive my mother to the edge and cause my dad to wonder if I'd like to stop for a while to make some ice cream.

When the door of Mr. Gobracht's cabin opened, I saw a short, round man with a wide head and wrinkled white skin wearing a formal black suit, white shirt, black string tie, and black vest with a gold chain. He had bushy white eyebrows over ice-blue eyes that were magnified by eyeglasses perched on his nose. He did not smile.

He waved me to the piano bench, flipped open some Mozart, and said with a German accent, "Let me hear you play, jah?"

With trepidation, I sat down, scanned the music, and attacked the keys.

"Ach, you sound like a dog walking on a drum. Like this."

He sat beside me, showed me the fingering and the rhythm, and then let me play. After a half-hour, he sent me home with a note folded and sealed with red wax. Walking home I could not figure out how to break open the seal, read the note, and reseal it without stirring suspicion.

Mom read it and looked at me with resignation. "He says no hope exists for you as a piano player and that I should save my money for better things."

That ended my piano playing.

When Mr. Gobracht conducted the Fairbanks Community Band, he mounted a podium with a baton that I came to know well. It appeared to be made of ironwood or ebony, about a foot long, three-quarters of an inch wide at its base, and a quarter-inch wide at its silver-capped tip.

When I oomphed or pahed my tuba microseconds off the beat, or blew one-billionth of a note off key, Mr. Gobracht would glare at me and stop the band. "With my baton, not against it, Herr de Yonge," he said. "On key, if you please . . . after me . . ."

Mr. Gobracht offered no second chances. The next time I erred, he fired the baton at my forehead. It was a formidable missile. CLANG! The baton banged off the tuba's bell, which I had pushed in front of my face at the last second, provoking laughter from my fellow musicians.

Mr. Gobracht glared, right hand extended, palm cupped, waiting for me to fetch his baton. Embarrassed, I walked forward to hand him his stick while the rest of the band accompanied me with an obbligato of haw-haws, except for the drummer, who accompanied my steps with subtle brushes on the snare drum.

I credit Mr. Gobracht with helping me to reach two fundamental understandings: first, I was an appreciator of music, not a musician, and second, music must be excellent or it is nothing. In music, how hard you sweat means naught. It's what you produce that matters.

My mother, bless her heart, clung to the belief that if I practiced enough I would overcome my musical shortcomings. She may have been right. But the truth is that I didn't have the will to practice when an exciting book lay at hand, or a baseball game beckoned, or there were fish to catch and grouse to hunt.

Twenty-eight

HATLESS JOE AND HIS FERRETS

"Hatless Joe" lived near us, on Hall Street. He earned his nickname because he never wore a hat, no matter how hot or how cold the weather. I thrilled anytime I saw Hatless Joe, with his dozen rat terriers trotting along beside him, pushing a wooden-wheeled cart up Wendell toward Mort Cass's warehouse.

Mort Cass ran a grocery at Fourth and Cushman. He was the father of my friend, Morty. The Casses lived a half-block down Wendell from us, next to the Burnettes. In the huge Cass backyard, which ran down to the willows along the Chena, was a big mustard-colored warehouse. Once, it had received goods directly from paddle-wheel steamboats on the river. Now, trucks delivered food supplies there.

The steamboats that founded and fed Fairbanks for decades before the railroad bled away their commerce also had delivered to the banks of the Chena a thriving population of a species likely to outlive humans—*rattus norvegicus*—the Norway Rat. Hatless Joe made a living ridding houses, stores, and warehouses of these nasty immigrants, which were known to run as much as twenty inches from their heads to the tips of their tails.

In Joe's cart were cages of ferrets. As he trundled along, Morty and I and every boy within a half mile fell in behind him with bats and clubs.

Hatless Joe made sure that no cars were parked anywhere near the warehouse. He wanted a clear killing field. He personally checked inside the warehouse to ensure all humans had departed the premises. Then, he carried cages of male ferrets inside and set those fierce predators loose. Finally, he latched the last door closed and with hand signals and whistles stationed his terriers around the warehouse. We boys deployed with them, cudgels ready. At first nothing happened. The terriers rambled nervously, whining and yapping and alert. Boys called back and forth, expectant. Hatless Joe prowled with a stout stick of the kind Friar Tuck used to get Robin Hood's attention.

After what seemed like hours, the dogs' ears perked and we heard squeaking, scuffling, and screams from inside as the ferrets raced with flashing razor teeth through holes and rat tunnels. A blackish-brown rat squirted in panic from the warehouse. A terrier lunged. The rat ran. The terrier grabbed the rat from behind the neck, shaking it like an old rag. The rat squealed, coughed blood, its legs thrashing, and went limp. The terrier dropped it, its muzzle red from blood, and went looking for another prey. A second rat raced out of the warehouse. Another dog nailed it. Then came another rat, then pairs of rats, and finally bunches of rats. The terriers raced after them and so did the boys. We clubbed what the dogs missed, especially wounded rats trying to creep away into the bushes with broken spines.

By then, dozens of panicked rats were running every which way. The terriers dripped rat blood as did the boys' shoes and pants—stains our mothers would make us pay for with lashings later. But we didn't care. Blood lust conquered all.

In the melee, Hatless Joe stumped around. His stick never missed. One swing equaled one dead rat, cracked over the spine in full stride. As he walked, Joe also stooped, grabbed a dead rat by the tail, and tossed it into a growing pile of dead rats.

The slaughter lasted an hour. When no more rats raced from the warehouse, Joe whistled in the terriers, watered and washed them, and wiped them down with towels from the cart. We boys helped pile up the dead rats and posed beside them.

When the job was done, Joe removed a metal box from the cart. In it was a female ferret in heat. He put her in a cage and put the cage inside the warehouse. Her smell would allure the male ferrets to abandon sating themselves on rat meat and to rush to her. One by one, Joe collected, wiped down, and caged the aroused male ferrets. Sometimes he came up a ferret or two short and that saddened him. The rats, when cornered, would fight. Not every ferret would survive.

Hatless Joe told us that he was paid by the job, not by the rat, but his service included hauling off the rat carcasses. Hatless skinned them out. He sold the good pelts. The carcasses, well . . . we speculated about that. He said he fed the rats to the dogs.

Yet, nobody ever saw Hatless Joe buying meat.

Twenty-nine

CHARLIE MAIN'S WONDERMENTS STORE

I learned to do business with Charlie Main, a tall, flabby man who usually needed a shave. Charlie and his thin, elderly wife ran a combination store and boarding house at First and Noble, a two-story log building catty-corner to Greimann's Bus depot and garage.

A few small hanging bulbs illuminated the display cases, shelves, and drawers in Charlie's store. The store contained countless delights—toys, trinkets, jewelry, watches, pens, slingshots, mummified squirrels in jars, campaign buttons, military insignia, new and second hand tools, and much more. Charlie also sold furs, ivory tusks, and ivory that Charlie said had been carved by Eskimo artists into jewelry, cribbage boards, and chessboards.

Often, full pelts of timber wolves hung outside, heads attached, eyes closed, teeth showing, against the tall dirty panes of the store's windows. A variety of fox pelts dangled in rows inside, strung on wires. So did martin (sable), mink, and ermine skins, and coyote hides. In one corner were a pile of coyote tails for making parka ruffs and little piles of squirrel pelts. Charlie also bought and stacked rolls of urine-tanned moose and caribou leather that he bought from Indians. The store smelled of Charlie's pipe smoke; hides; camphor, used for insect repellant; moth balls, and curry, which Charlie's wife often cooked for her boarders—all creating a palpable invasion on the nostrils.

Dad told me that Charlie would buy rabbit pelts. So I skinned out the snowshoe hares I snared. Charlie gave me fifty cents apiece for each good hide, which he judged by fingering the underside and the fur.

One day, biking out the Steese Highway to the Fox gold-dredging operation, I came upon a live red fox in the road, its back broken from having been hit by a car. Its head was unmarked. In those days, women wore fox pelts around their necks with eyeless head skins still attached. The fox looked at me for mercy. I conked it dead with a rock and skinned it by the road with my jackknife, careful to scrape all the meat from the hide. Otherwise yellow jackets would swarm me if they smelled decaying flesh.

Buzz accompanied me that day, finally able to keep up on his bike. I rolled the fox pelt, tied it to my bicycle seat, and we rode onto Engineer Creek, where men blasted surrounding hillsides with huge, powerful hydraulic hoses in advance of a Fairbanks Exploration Company dredge. The water ripped away dirt in torrents of mud that washed into the creek. The ripping exposed bedrock and ancient placer gravels—fodder for dredge buckets that would tear up rocks and soil and drop them into the maw of the dredge. It floated along a few feet every hour on a pond that it created itself. It devoured the landscape twenty-four hours a day. The hydraulics also washed out bare fossils and sometimes entire carcasses of mastodons and other critters that had lived and died there eons earlier. Buzz and I sought mastodon tusks that the F.E. workers stacked into piles.

In our saddlebags, we carried hacksaws, gunny sacks, and rope. We could sell the mastodon ivory to Charlie Main for one dollar a pound if its ringed layers, like the rings in a tree, hadn't separated. The working stiffs didn't care if we sorted through the pile to find the best tusks so long as we didn't make a mess and stayed out of the way. A dead kid, one man told me with a smile, is a pain in the ass because of all the paper that would have to be filled out.

After a little practice, I could tell by looking and hefting if a tusk was tight. Most of the tusks I could barely lift, except with a shoulder under them. If the ivory looked good, we'd hacksaw off pieces about two feet long, big enough for polishing and carving. Good antique ivory is heavy. After Buzz and I had gathered about twenty pounds for him and thirty pounds for me, we put the pieces into sacks and tied them to our bikes for the long ride back into town.

I had no intention of giving Mom all that Charlie paid us. Charlie and I had an understanding. I would bring goods. We'd deal. He'd pay, in cash. Nothing was said to anyone.

Thirty

DOING A MAN'S JOB

The summer I turned thirteen, I did not understand the significance of my father, then sixty-seven, walking home early one day from the N.C. with a black and blue cheek.

He'd been in a fistfight at work, he told my mother as she rushed to make a cold pack to put on his face. He named a much younger hardware clerk who had worked at the N.C. for a few months. "The other guy looks worse," he joked, wincing.

When Mom had calmed down, he delivered the bad news. Les Almquist, manger of the hardware department and a good friend, had laid Dad off for a month or two and had fired the other clerk, both for fighting.

My mother asked the natural question, "What did you fight over?"

"You don't want to know," my Dad said. In our house, that was that.

Mom began to cry. We couldn't afford for Dad not to work.

"Easy, Eva," Dad said. "Bill Hunter's given me a job in the meantime."

Bill Hunter, Dad's closest friend, ran the N.C. power plant, which was attached to the store. The power plant was a fiefdom all to itself in the N.C. organization. Bill Hunter's office, just a few feet away from the roar of the turbines, became an informal club for Dad and others, including Jess Rust, who also worked for Hunter. After the N.C. closed at 6 p.m., Hunter pulled a bottle of whiskey out of his desk drawer to enliven these evening gatherings. They usually lasted about twenty or thirty minutes, just enough time, as Dad liked to say, "to get two legs"—to knock down two drinks to walk home on.

Dad soon asked whether I'd like to do some work down at the power plant. I hastened to consent. I felt I was becoming a man among men.

To my surprise, I discovered that my father was not helping Jess Rust and others monitor and operate the turbines that supplied the town with all of its electricity. No, Rust led me to the furnace room, where I found my dad and a man I didn't know stripped to the waist, sweat pouring off of them, shoveling coal into the furnace's roaring flames.

Dad greeted me but didn't bother to explain: a paying job was a paying job.

And I had one if I wanted it, Rust said. The furnace room had two furnaces in it. One was cold, shut down for maintenance, he said.

"And your job would be"—he bent down and opened a grate under the furnace—"to crawl under there and rip out the asbestos. See that gray wadding there? Rip down the asbestos, bring it out, and put it in this sack. Fifty cents an hour." The temporary job would take a few days.

Just then, Dad pulled open the other furnace door again and the heat blasted us. Dad and the other man again shoveled coal into the flaming maw.

Rust looked at me for an answer. So did Dad. Though I hated small spaces, I was ashamed to say no.

I said I would be glad to do the work. My Dad nodded. Jess Rust nodded. That was that. Ignorance is not bliss, but it certainly is a comfort.

I began right away. Taking off my shirt, I crawled into a space about three feet high under the cold furnace. I reached up and grabbed hold of the heavy gray asbestos. It gave way, crumbling into pieces, and a cloud of dust fell onto my face.

I coughed and choked for the rest of the day, except for lunch, sharing half of my dad's Spam sandwich during his half-hour break. It was hard, sweaty, nasty work. I was caked with asbestos, which made me itch. Soon my armpits felt as if they had been sandpapered. At the end of the day, I joined Dad and the other man in a big shower to wash off as much asbestos as possible.

Mom threw a fit when she saw my clothes, but shut up at a word from Dad.

"Johnnie and I are too tired to listen to this," he said. "He worked like a man. Respect that."

I worked for weeks under that furnace. Dad and I walked to work together. We shared lunch together. We showered up. We walked home. For decades later I waited for the first signs that all the asbestos I breathed under that furnace would bring on lung cancer. No signs yet. Dumb luck.

Thirty-one

BOYHOOD'S END

As an overweight, slow-footed high-school freshman in 1948, I was a poor basketball player, compared to Al Baumeister and Bob Burglin. In Fairbanks High School, basketball was the only game that counted. I didn't count. Worse, I had poor body strength. Gym classes became a horror.

Failure as an athlete channeled me to exceed as a student. My brain was quick, agile even. Without much forethought, I labored to excel and soon ranked among the first in academics. Alas, then as now, to be only a leading student in an American high school conferred no great status. I preferred popularity to grades but got only the grades. I wanted girls to reciprocate my lust but found myself feeling and acting like a klutz, and this defined how others saw me. I suffered that terrible disease—juvenile anxiety.

Then, our family suffered a profound blow. While walking home, Dad slipped on the ice and cracked his right hip. He was sixty-eight. Alone on Wendell Avenue in the winter darkness, he dragged himself home, drenched with sweat from the effort and agonizing pain. He pounded on the door until my mother came and, with an exclamation of fear, pulled Dad inside and helped him into his chair. His groan summoned me and Buzz from the shed. Mom and I pulled off Dad's outdoor clothes, lifted him up, and helped him into the bedroom, where he laid down in great pain.

Sick leave and health insurance did not exist in Fairbanks unless you had a government job. At the N.C. you used vacation time for days you stayed home sick. After that, your pay stopped. The next day, Dad staggered to work on a cane. Buzz and I walked with him on our way to school. Each time he put weight on the foot, he snorted in pain. At the N.C., I saw frozen sweat on his coat collar. We left him there, white-faced, explaining to Les Almquist, a sympathetic man, what had happened.

Soon the pain forced him to stay home and get medical help. No operation existed then to fix a cracked hip. Doc Haggland gave Dad a half-pint of morphine pills. There was nothing else for him but rest. This meant the family income would dwindle. After a couple of weeks, Dad went back to work. Now and then, he would chew a morphine tablet he kept in an Anacin tin. His injured leg shrank. John Contento, a young shoemaker, built up the sole and heel on Dad's right shoe so that his foot would touch the ground. Dad's fishing and hunting days were over. He knew it and suffered the loss without complaint. Unlike my mother and me, Harry de Yonge was stoic. He never bitched. He never spread his pain to others to enjoy. He continued working and did the best he could.

My mother found me a job working in Contento's Family Shoe store on Cushman Street. John and his wife, Eleanor, both working people, appreciated our family's situation.

The Contento family took me on as a stock boy, replenishing shelves with boxes of shoes, cleaning floors, dusting windows, and tending to shoe displays. I had no time to sell newspapers. I worked after school from four to six and all day Saturdays. Alas, the Contentos paid by check, which Eleanor made out to my mother. My spending money all but disappeared. Mom, meanwhile, went back to work as a secretary.

After I had worked at the store for a while, John Contento, a savvy businessman, taught me how to sell shoes, how to size up customers for fit, style, quality, and price. John treated me like a younger brother. Round-faced with bulging blue eyes and a gut that hung over sharply creased whipcord slacks and shined shoes, Contento always had a lit 1886 cigar in hand or in an ashtray nearby. In those days, stores provided ashtrays and spittoons for customers and employees alike. John also taught me to shine shoes, price shoes, keep records, and create displays. Now and then, he would slip me a five-dollar bill and say, "Jack, get yourself a good haircut, for God's sake."

Although work cut into study time, my desire to excel helped me to maintain my grades. One winter, I won the radio quiz, "Young Alaska Speaks," created by Al Bramstad, manager of KFAR radio. In the final show, which was broadcast live, I defeated Ron Nerland, one of our town's brightest students. Ron's family owned a furniture store and other property and was active in Interior Alaska politics.

I cannot remember the final question, but I still feel the thrill of victory. I received the magnificent prize of one hundred dollars from the hand of Austin E. Lathrop, then one of Alaska's few resident millionaires, who owned a chain of Alaska radio stations and movie theaters; the Suntrana coal mine near Healy; commercial and apartment buildings; and the newspaper I had peddled—the *Fairbanks Daily News-Miner.* "Cap" Lathrop, as he was known, was a squared-off runt mean to his employees and anti-union, anti-tax, anti-government, anti Roosevelt, and a penny-pincher. Therefore, other business worthies, politicians, and the general population admired him extravagantly. His praises flowed from the editors of his newspaper. He hated the idea of statehood for Alaska. A state government, he feared, would exert much more power than Alaska's weak territorial government dominated by the U.S. Department of the Interior. Lathrop was in his eighties when he handed me one hundred silver dollars in brown-paper rolls. A year later, a rolling railroad car at his coal mine struck him and killed him.

The money went to my mother for deposit in the family bank account. Given my father's condition, my parents now squirreled away every extra cent. At the time, ungrateful wretch that I was, I did not appreciate their need. I did appreciate that my victory as Mr. Smarts elevated my status in high school by zero percent.

The next year, Dad's pain from a badly mending hip grew worse. Forced retirement loomed. His leg kept shrinking. He could not walk without his cane. He no longer could climb a ladder, a necessity for a clerk working the high-ceiling layout of the N.C. hardware's storage areas. Slowed even more by his dragging leg, he had to take special care walking on ice and snow and be sure to allow plenty of time for crossing the street. Falling to rebreak that hip or to break the other hip would ruin the family. Mother talked about that all the time.

Thanks to Franklin Roosevelt's New Deal, Dad at sixty-nine would get Social Security, but it was not enough to live on in Fairbanks with its high prices, certainly not for a family of four. Mom still had seventeen years to go before she qualified for Social Security. Neither of them would get, or expected, a pension from the N.C. or any of Mom's sundry employers.

Economic necessity, as usual, ruled. My parents decided to quit Fairbanks and head south to California, home of Dad's brother Jack; sisters Dora, Etta, and Lou; and Mom's mother and sister. Fairbanks' cost of living ran twenty-five to thirty percent higher than the Lower 48. California was warm. Cheap fruit and produce abounded, as did seafood. Medical care was more accessible, and more affordable, and specialists could be found at the major medical schools. My parents were not happy to go. Fairbanks had been their home for nearly fifty years. All their friends lived in Fairbanks. So did most of their memories. Both of them talked about how hard it was saying goodbye to people you knew would stand by you and help you in bad times.

In June 1950, after my sophomore year, the de Yonges listed their log cabin for sale, sold and gave away household and personal goods, and shipped to Uncle Jack's place in Felton, California our clothing, weapons, and books and mementoes too dear to surrender.

Dad and Mom bought with their savings a new gray, four-door 1948 Plymouth with a stick shift. With the ten percent N.C. employee discount, it cost them eight hundred dollars. Dad gave me driving lessons. Mom did not know how to drive. Despite not having a driver's license, I would be the main driver on our exodus south down the rough Alaska Highway through the Yukon Territory and on to Alberta, Montana, Wyoming, Washington, Oregon, and northern California. Dad rarely drove because of his leg. But he did take the wheel when we passed through towns, fearing that we might be stopped by police. We hit the road on a sunny June morning, the four of us and Tip, scrunched among our tightly packed belongings. Our spare tires (we would need those) were lashed to the rear bumper and to a rack on top. Nobody saw us off. Neighbors, friends, and co-workers already had said their farewells. The log cabin had sold for a trifle and now belonged to a stranger. With dust welling behind us, we rolled as a family for the last time down Wendell Avenue, cut up Lacey to Gaffney Road, and soon were heading south on the Richardson Highway.

I did not know then, and did not appreciate until months later, that although my body had left Fairbanks, my soul had not—not yet.

EPILOGUE

The greatest danger on the Alaska Highway in 1950 was not hitting a moose but more likely running into a stalled truck on a curve, perhaps a junker from Alabama piled with watermelons to peddle door to door in Fairbanks. The arrival of watermelons from across the country into what Alaskans still fondly call the "Last Frontier" signified that the frontier life we lived was slipping away. The frontier no longer was remote. Every day, the new highway, the railroad, and commercial airliners deposited people, goods, and ideas that smelted old Fairbanks into a culture much like the rest of the United States.

The disappearance of the frontier ended a time warp on the edge of the wilderness where a bit of the Nineteenth Century dangled into the Twentieth Century. We had lived on a wrinkle in time's flow. Different times occurred simultaneously. I did not know then E.E. Cummings' lines, ". . . listen, there's a hell of a good universe next door; let's go." But I soon learned the meaning of it.

I had spent my boyhood in that universe next door—remote, proudly self-sufficient yet dependent on an alien place we called "the Outside." Most families killed a moose or a caribou to put meat on the table. We netted, fish-wheeled, speared, and dynamited salmon to satisfy the papal order of the day: eat fish on Friday. The Sears catalog dictated our fashions. Most of all, we talked about how special, how brave, how uplifting, how heroic it was to live in Alaska, where most of the time the weather was terrible but the scenery would be wonderful and one could be alone, really alone, with the forest creatures and with God. At the same time, bulldozers were blading the forest creatures and God out of the way.

After a hard journey, the de Yonges settled near Santa Cruz, where I grasped that the universe Outside moved to a different and faster clock. It confused me, and I had a hard time in a new high school. Clothing was different, manners were different, expectations were different, and opportunities for travel, culture, and mischief far exceeded anything I dreamed of in Fairbanks. I realized that my new classmates regarded me as a rural bumpkin. They were, by their lights, probably right.

I got into fights right away. Growing up in Fairbanks had welded in me an ethic that it is better to have fought and lost than never to have fought at all. I learned, though, that in Santa Cruz it was not unknown during a fight for a knife to flash. My father told me to run from a knife, charge a gun. I didn't run from a knife. But I made damn sure I stayed away from those with a reputation for using them. I spent more hours of school time fishing from the municipal dock in Santa Cruz, and dodging truant officers, than I spent in classes.

I hadn't understood that growing up in Fairbanks automatically admitted me into the society of Fairbanks High School. There, I wasn't much, but I was somebody. In Santa Cruz, not having grown up there made me a nobody, a classic outsider—a gloomy cuss with no friends except a few other suffering nobodies. Lonely, I became angry, hard to manage in school and hard to manage at home as, finally, manhood came to me and my body and temper vibrated with that most dangerous fuel known to humankind: testosterone. As my voice deepened and my muscles grew, so did my need to return to Fairbanks. Homesickness wracked me.

I flew north for a summer of selling shoes. The summer after, still seventeen, defiant and cursing California, I left my parents' home for good and flew north where I slipped back into that more comfortable universe beside the Chena River.

It was a puerile choice. Months of semi-poverty in Fairbanks taught me much. I came to see that chance—good luck, if you will—had given me youthful adventure in a wartime boom town. But now the boom was over. Living in Fairbanks was hardly different than living in Minot, North Dakota. Both became cold-winter outposts in the new Cold War. We feared nuclear war and an end to federal handouts but didn't know which would be worse. I devoured books and grudgingly sensed that the world had more to offer than this little town at the end of the Alaska Highway. Even so, I stayed, scrimped along. It was better to have some friends than none. Because Al Baumeister and other pals were enrolling at the then one-and-only University of Alaska, five miles away in the hamlet of College, I signed up, too, to see if learned professors could scrape away my bumpkinhood and maybe teach me which fork to use. And grayling fishing was still good in the long summer evenings.

I look back now with amused fondness. As I write, I listen to a Rachmaninov prelude that I first heard when Miss Weller played it on her portable wind-up phonograph for us little savages in her fifth-grade class. I can see her now, her bunned hair nodding and smiling in sympathetic rhythm with the beautiful piano music pouring out of the little speaker. I know she enjoyed these musical moments, if only because her nasty little charges had to shut up for a while.

Soon, with a goblet of lemonade and gin, a palliative prescribed by my father for most of the world's ills, I will listen to a Louis Armstrong set that first thrilled me from a screen on a machine in the Silver Dollar Bar, a stinking, smoke-filled saloon where bartenders swung baseball bats to break up fights between patrons seeking a hooker's favor. Between fistfights, I watched jazz bands on a movie screen if I could cajole a boozer to clink a silver dollar into the machine. Bless those drunks generous to a wheedling, ten-year-old newsboy.

Today, most of Fairbanks looks like Sprawl Anywhere, U.S.A. Yet, remnants of my boyhood remain. Long ago abandoned by the bureaucrats, lawyers, and judges, the old Federal Building still stands at Second and Cushman. On Second Avenue, the Co-Op is a pale shadow of the drugstore and fountain it once was. The Mecca Bar still turns out drinks in a dark, cavernous gloom unchanged over all those years. A few blocks west, a few familiar Cowles Street neighborhoods survive. Amid big birches and cottonwoods stand many frame houses and a few ancient log cabins, mostly swaybacked with age, built by the first stampeders.

Wendell Avenue, alas, now functions as a bleak arterial. It feeds traffic over the Chena River on a concrete bridge built where the Heman boys once ruled in ice castles they built among the willows. The willows are long gone, bulldozed. Where the winos camp now I don't know. And where do couples canoodle outdoors of a summer's night?

The de Yonge manse, like all the log cabins in our block, long ago disappeared. The whole neighborhood has vanished.

And the people in it have vanished, too, except in memory.

We, too, shall soon cease. At the thought, I wipe away a small tear and reach for my gin and lemonade, listen to Louis Armstrong become Gabriel on the trumpet, and think of my mother and dad and brother Buzz and Tip and Hatless Joe and Burning Daylight, Catcher's Mitt Charlie, Nick the Greek, No Nose Nellie, Dynamite Red, Mrs. Ford, and all the others. I wonder what happened to all those Russian pilots who survived the war. Did Stalin really shoot them? And damn it, why do I lack absolute proof that Will Rogers, the night before he died, cuddled me in his arms?

INDEX

F

G

H

I

J

K

ABOUT THE AUTHOR

JACK DE YONGE (also known as John, Jackie, and names too gamey to be published here) is an Alaskan who lives in Washington State, "but only because I can fly fish here the year around," he says.

Born, reared, and educated in Fairbanks, he graduated from the University of Alaska with ten dollars and a Babe Ruth candy bar in his pocket. He learned the newspaper trade at the Fairbanks *Daily News-Miner* and, after Army service, moved to Seattle where he weaseled an M.A. degree in English from the University of Washington.

Hunger caused him to hire onto the *Seattle Times*, where, as an arts critic, he enjoyed having free tickets to every theater event in town, which sweetened his social life. For some years after marrying Sonjia Urseth, another writer and reader, de Yonge taught and administered at an Eastern Washington community college. By then he was involving himself in Democratic politics and the environmental movement.

The excitement of newspapering lured him back to a reporting job at what he calls "the best newspaper ever published in Washington State," the *Seattle Post-Intelligencer*, where he also served as an editor and columnist. During a leave of absence from the paper, he became executive director of the Alaska Statehood Commission at a time when federal interventions troubled Alaskans. He ran his own consulting firm for decades, with an interval during which he helped elect Mike Lowry governor of Washington and served Lowry as a speechwriter and advisor on natural resources.

De Yonge counts among his greatest achievements helping to get the Skagit River system in Washington State set off under the U.S. Wild and Scenic Rivers Act and in helping to persuade President Bill Clinton to preserve the Hanford Reach of the Columbia River from robbers, rapers, and spoilers by creating the Hanford Reach National Monument.

Now retired and living with his wife beside the Skagit River, de Yonge alternates between visiting his favorite fly-fishing areas and visiting his favorite doctors for repairs. He attributes his long life to a social life devoid of prissies, prigs, and prudes.

RECOMMENDATIONS FOR READERS

seeking to learn more about Alaska's history, culture, and way of life through biographies and memoirs of notable Alaskans.

ACCIDENTAL ADVENTURER
Memoir of the First Woman to Climb Mt. McKinley
Barbara Washburn, paperback, $16.95

ALASKA BLUES
A Story of Freedom, Risk, and Living Your Dream
Joe Upton, paperback, $14.95

ARCTIC BUSH PILOT
From Navy Combat to Flying Alaska's Northern Wilderness
James "Andy" Anderson & Jim Rearden, paperback, $17.95

COLD STARRY NIGHT
An Artist's Memoir
Claire Fejes, paperback, $17.95

NORTH TO WOLF COUNTRY
My Life among the Creatures of Alaska
James W. Brooks, paperback, $16.95

ON THE EDGE OF NOWHERE
Jim Huntington & Lawrence Elliott, paperback, $14.95

ONE SECOND TO GLORY
The Adventures of Iditarod Champion Dick Mackey
Lew Freedman, paperback, $16.95

RAISING OURSELVES
A Gwitch'in Coming of Age Story from the Yukon River
Velma Wallis, paperback, $14.95

RIDING THE WILD SIDE OF DENALI
Julie & Miki Collins, paperback, $14.95

SISTERS
Coming of Age & Living Dangerously in the Wild Copper River Valley
Samme Gallaher & Aileen Gallaher, paperback, $14.95

SPIRIT OF THE WIND
The Story of George Attla, Alaska's Legendary Sled Dog Racer
George Attla with Lew Freedman, paperback, $14.95

TALES OF ALASKA'S BUSH RAT GOVERNOR
The Extraordinary Autobiography of Jay Hammond, Wilderness Guide and Reluctant Politician
Jay Hammond, paperback, $17.95

SURVIVING THE ISLAND OF GRACE
Life on the Wild Edge of America
Leslie Leyland Field
paperback, $17.95

These titles can be found at or special-ordered from your local bookstore. A wide assortment of Alaska books also can be ordered directly from the publisher's website, **www.EpicenterPress.com**, or by calling 1-800-950-6663 day or night.

ALASKA BOOK ADVENTURES™
Epicenter Press
www.EpicenterPress.com